LIVING IN LOTUS LAND

LIVING IN LOTUS LAND

A Narrative Poem

J. R. PHILLIPS

ILLUMINA PRESS
PASADENA

Printed by Illumina Press
in the United States of America

ISBN 13: 978-1-7331119-5-9

Library of Congress Control Number Pending

Illumina Press Inc.
P.O BOX 60444,
Pasadena, CA 91116
626-460-7090

http://www.illuminapress.org

For **B. H. Fairchild**
& all the story-telling poets

CONTENTS

INTRODUCTION

In attempting to come to terms with J.R. Phillips' astonishing—and astonishingly ambitious—poem, *Living in Lotus Land,* I am embarrassed to recall myself at the age of nineteen standing in the shade of one of the neo-Mediterranean buildings in the very heart of Beat-era Venice Beach and thinking, "Gee, I should stay here for awhile and *write the great L.A. poem.*" And I had been in town only three days. J.R. Phillips has lived his entire life in and across the city of Los Angeles, from the working class through various layers of the middle class, through the interesting, complex Fifties (now reduced to cliché by Hollywood itself) and exotic Sixties and decade-stereotyped years since then, emerging in the present with one gnawing, obsessive, dream-racked question: "What *IS* Los Angeles?" And he certainly isn't the first writer to ask that question of his home city in order to discover himself.

As ludicrous as it might sound to those who haven't lived in L.A. long enough to feel, like Phillips, that they are somehow genetically attached to the city, it would nevertheless be fair to say that Los Angeles is Phillips' Alexandria. That is not to say that Phillips is L.A.'s Cavafy, though certainly he has embraced his city, loved it, hated it, struggled with it, absorbed it as much as Cavafy did his. In the section of *Living in Lotus Land* where Phillips speaks eloquently of that great L.A. institution, the dive bar, I can even sense the presence of Cavafy in the shadows sipping not ouzo but a cool gin and tonic, and seeing the floating slice of lime as a bikini-wrapped body in a Bel-Air swimming pool.

i

But this is not the voice of an academic historian. This is the voice of an author who experienced first-hand not only the most impactful events that affected the evolution of his city but possessed an equally impactful effect on the country at large. Everything from the relocation of the Dodgers, the Watts riots, the post-war aerospace boom, the drug addled '60s, the love-ins, the sexual revolution, the demoralization of Vietnam is artfully revisited, skillfully recaptured in a melodic sensibility.

From childhood to adulthood— fifty to sixty years of lightning paced changes that mirror a poet's adaptability against a city's rapid transformation from orange groves and desert skies to a megalopolis of enormous wealth and global influence.

It's all here from Disneyland to the Playboy mansion. From scenic racetracks and garden oasis to sunny beaches and bikini clad nymphets.

Living in Lotus Land is not a modern epic; on the other hand, it is not simply a memoir in verse. But it is the city-as-poem. In fact, if L.A. could write a poem about itself, extending over the past sixty years and filtered through a single consciousness, I think this might be it.

B.H. Fairchild

PREFACE

It's the Mid-1980s, I had been experimenting with the idea for a memoir in verse-form that would link the growth and development of the city I had lived in since I was four with my own personal development and growth. Perhaps influenced by my reading of Williams' *Paterson,* and greatly taken in by Rexroth's *The Dragon and the Unicorn* I fired off twenty-five beginning segments and shared them with a few friends and the novelist Gore Vidal who had been a client of mine while I was engaged in my banking career at Merrill Lynch. Gore, while admitting a preference for prose, commented, "I see a poem here with epic proportions and epic hurdles along the way. He smiled. "Good luck with that. You'll need it."

It's now some thirty years later, Gore is gone, my friends engaged in non-literary pursuits, and I have to ask myself is there even an audience for such an ambitious undertaking? The long poem or serial poem whether in sequential style of a Berryman's *Dream Songs* or the fragmented style of Eliot's *Waste Land* or Pound's *Cantos* has many detractors. As Nerys Williams once remarked in his essay titled "The Monstrosity of the Long Poem: "Writing 'long poems' in an age that has a capacious appetite for the image, a diminished attention span and a desire for the quick sound bite might seem counterintuitive, if not spectacularly naive." Or as Dr. Samuel Johnson once remarked of Milton's grand epic *Paradise Lost* "who would ever have wished it longer"?

Of course, this commentary begs the question: Does American poetry *in any form* have an audience? Poetry, its roots sourced in the story-telling tradition of ancient Greece and Rome, left that tradition with the advent of Modern and Post-Modern free verse and an emerging emphasis of text on the page. Over the years the story telling tradition of poetry has taken a back-seat to the preponderance of linguistic gymnastics and stylistic experimentation. Outside of the light verse of a Ogden Nash or the cerebral humor of a Dorothy Parker or a Billy Collins, poetry as a medium for popular affirmation has been superseded by folk-rock aficionados like Dylan and Leonard Cohen or the sub-culture phenomenon of Hip-Hop and caustic urban Rapp.

Faced with this most obvious of realities, why then this futile attempt at a long poem concerning of all places, this heartland of crass materialism, gross commercialization, and a reputation of a culture devoid of any remarkable identity except that of being the chief exporter of celluloid fantasies? Indeed, it is this latter reality, this popular association of Los Angeles with the flickering images cast upon theatre screens around the world that has captured the hearts and minds of the world's population and has transformed this desert wilderness into a sort of mirage of bikini-clad beach nymphs, palm-lined boulevards, expensive cars and houses the size of great royal palaces. This allurement toward things illusory and fantastic, this neverland narcotic of palm trees, movie sets and rolling mountains has drawn so many to these shores, critics and historians alike have equated this often fatal attraction to the mythical land of the lotus depicted in Homer's Odyssey.

So why not revisit Poetry's roots? Return back to the traditions of story-telling and myth-making? Certainly Los Angeles, for that matter California itself—has all the ingredients of mythical intrigue and archetypal allusions. Such allusions seem an obvious source for inspiration to a poet seeking to connect the events and images that constitute his life's experiences to the environment which frames these perceptions and provides some sort of insight into what these events and images convey.

So why a poem? (Assuming this effort satisfies such a distinction). Why not a short-story or a novel or a drama? Certainly the likes of Raymond Chandler, John Fante, Nathaniel West, or Scott Fitzgerald, were more than adequately suited to the task. Yet outside of a handful of pseudo-Beat actors and a few local workshop facilitators, few poets of real distinction come to mind—even Bukowski, seems more recognized as a novelist— that have made effective use of the underlying mythology of this town. The mythological aspect of L.A has always seemed to me as obvious as a child's belief in Santa Claus and the easter bunny.

This wide-spread acceptance of Los Angeles as a fantasy dreamland of palm trees, sunshine, and endless beaches, this ubiquitous Mecca for the poor and the downtrodden, this perpetual playground for the rich and the famous is so deeply rooted in our American Myth that it screams out for the kind of highly structured, highly descriptive literary art form that only the intensity and musical vitality of poetry can provide. Rightly or wrongly, this was the path I chose, this was the journey I attempted to articulate in verse.

J. R. Phillips
Los Angeles, California
June 14, 2014

LIVING IN LOTUS LAND

...that a man in himself is a city,
beginning, seeking, achieving, and concluding his life
in ways which the various aspects of a city may
embody—if imaginatively conceived—any city, all the
details of which may be made to voice his most
intimate convictions.

—William Carlos Williams

The city, half-imagined (yet wholly real),
begins and ends in us, roots lodged in
memory.

—Lawrence Durrell,
The Alexandria Quartet

I

EVEN from the airplane,
the songs of Sirens rise from the water.
The water below
beaded by sunlight, shimmers diamond-like
on a million backyard swimming pools.
We are lured by the lotus
rising from the chlorine.
The passenger beside me
is dazzled by the myriad of mirrors
replicating the rolling terrain
in glaring green patches
and houses like tiny toy boxes.

We have left behind New York,
the Ithaca Homer never knew:
cold gray skies, a brown-stone campus,
a conference in tribute
to an exiled pedophile from Russia,
Pushkin admirer, avid butterfly collector.
Cold gray skies, a land suitable only to the esoteric,
devotees of the arcane and the mummified consensus
of Eliot and Pound.

"Questo è il paradiso o l'inferno?"
The passenger beside me speaks
as we begin our descent.

A funny man,

                  a Florentine I suspect,

with the name *Beatrice* tattooed across his wrist.

I am reading a book about a man returning home

from a journey.

The man beside me suggests I dress lightly.

You can see the heat waves quivering

along the pavement below.

He reminds me how oppressive the heat can be

when we make our descent.

He seems to be an expert on that subject.

From the tiny porthole of the plane's fuselage:

Miles and miles of asphalt arteries,

long winding rivers of metal membranes,

dry mountains and desolate deserts,

a bright sparkling ocean,

the sun skipping across the sea like polished stone.

And the sky, a curtain of clouds

dissolving into glass our narrow porthole.

Everywhere motion and movement,

everywhere swimming pools and freeways,

parking lots and car dealerships,

housing tracts, factories, office buildings,

golf resorts, boneyards and junkyards,

a world of rust-colored mist, of careening crowds

where space and privacy is overwhelmed
and solace is a luxury reserved for the privileged few.

As Vidal said to me, circa 1982,
"Imagine this land if a sprinkler system
ever shut down."
The first "literati" to run for local office,
(the word "literati" preferred over "gay"
or "sexually ambiguous" in a letter dated 10/23/88)
and Rexroth, that loud bombastic man
decrying: "All this mass of humanity and no center,
no center of focus."

Looping through the Mulholland Bridge underpass,
veering down the Highland corridor
a taxi-cab pauses, traffic grinding to a halt,
our vision suddenly fixed
on the luster of light from bleached-white buildings,
a Hollywood skyline of palm trees,
department store signs, a recording studio
designed to look like a stack of vinyl records,
movie palaces the scale of castles…
And it's 1957, sister and I in the back seat
of a 1955 Buick Roadmaster,
brother up front, Uncle Bud at the wheel.
Three of us: wide-eyed refugees
from the stilted, sterile confines
of a rural San Fernando Valley.

My six-year-old sister: "Maybe we'll see a movie-star."
My eleven-year-old brother: "Look there!
I'll bet we can find one at The Carolina Pines."
And eight-year-old me, silent,
mesmerized by space & time,
journeys that lift us above the mundane,
that transcend the ordinary, the common.

Dear adventurous Uncle Bud,
a recent migrant from the dingy dark decay
of a Midwest city fading to decline.
George, "Buddy", Lynch,
champion swimmer, horseman, world war survivor,
who could con Movie Moguls,
dine with dignitaries, charm the socks off landlords
to live rent-free in an upscale Hollywood apartment.
Dear dear Uncle Bud:
the bane and shame of his sister's only blood,
my mother.
A time when words like "bi-polar"or "obsessive compulsion",
were textbook terms tucked neatly away in book shelves
and academic fodder,
alien concerns to three wide-eyed urchins
in a 1950 world of Art Deco magic, movie theatre palaces,
restaurants in shapes of Dutch windmills
or gigantic Derby hats,
the flavor of urban refinement
nascent in sunshine luminance.

The taxi cab pauses and idles.
I stare out the window at the ghost of a diner
where the four of us once sat at a red vinyl booth
while overhead a miniature train on a track
circled continuously around our make-believe world.

II

Our make-believe world dissolves like opaque vapors
scattering above our heads as years, days, hours
hurl us back to solid ground.
You find yourself at the place where Wright
built his Hollyhock House.
It was the middle of summer and R. Deutsch
buried his brother the winter before.
The lines carved in stone traced an ancient Aztec pattern.
Olive trees and Eucalyptus remain
where an oil heiress envisioned a dream palace
in harmony with its native environs.

You find yourself alone near the ocean.
The sound of seagulls and rolling waves.
The aqua blue air in the afternoon sun
fragrant with the sea.
Tongues of white foam lick the shoreline.
Sirens and selkies appear on the rocks.

Circe whispers in your ear.

You lose yourself in senses and sounds:

No massive shopping malls, no promenades.

Sun-bleached bungalows, the Venice Beach boardwalk

with its concession booths, hot dog stands, and tattoo parlors,

the Avalon Ballroom where your parents went to dance.

It's 1959, Santa Monica. You discover pizza and cherry coke.

You enter the magical gateway of aquariums and roller coaster rides

And when the war came eight years later—the "head" shops,

 the happenings, sand castles for peace, Baez on the beach,

hippies staring in reverence…but that is a subject

for another chapter.

So much has changed.

But you keep returning, resurrecting this city

which buries its past.

"No one ever stays here too long,"

Dorothy Parker once remarked.

Faulkner called it a "necessary death".

We search everywhere for remnants and mementos:

1. The bar stool at Musso's where Fitzgerald wavered.
    (the room on Hayworth
    where he drank himself to death)
2. The Parva-Sed Apta on Ivar where Nathaniel West
    let loose the locusts from the hills
3. The house where Mann concocted Faustus after Schoenberg
4. 740 Kings Road where Huxley pondered the mystical

5. The Ambassador where Bobby was murdered
   —and to think the Coconut Grove once shimmered on the corner
6. The Hollywood Sign the studios abandoned
7. The vacant lots and bank buildings where once stood
   The Garden of Allah, the Hollywood Hotel, Trocadero,
   Mocambo, Earl Carrol's, Schwab's Drug, Montmarte, the Garden
   Apartments, Dolores' Drive In
8. Coroner's Case No. 81128: Norma Jean Baker, age 36, cause of
   death: probable suicide

Dylan T. arrived in the spring of '51,
D.T. got the d.t.'s from too much sun.

III

Too much sun but never enough to satisfy.
Sun and sea shore melodies dilate our eyes
and lure us westward towards the sound.
Sirens and selkies on a jagged reef,
a music that pulls us
toward the voluptuous waters,
Malibu, Santa Monica, Brentwood, Paradise Cove.
Islands of avarice and conspicuous consumption.
Everything always new, always in motion:
in pastel-painted mansions,
in green glowing manicured grass,

in Tiffany window displays,

in silver-plated trays of chocolate,

caviar, oysters, French Bistro Champagne.

A world of money.

Money in petrodollars and yen,

money in pesos and shekles and rubles.

Money in the hat of the street performer,

in the crack of the stripper.

Up and down the boulevard,

around every street corner

a whiff of it is always in the air.

They come from everywhere to find it,

whole generations.

They crawl across borders,

they climb the clouds, they sail and risk rough waters.

Looking out past twenty-two floors of office windows,

a radiant glow lights the Wilshire Corridor below.

It's as if the whole world emptied its bounties

on this little corner on the far edge of the Western divide.

All along the avenues:

Bentleys and Porsches, vintage Ferraris, Lamborghinis,

Maseratis, BMWs, Mercedes (the Volkswagon of Beverly Hills).

I think of my father on the assembly line at work,

sweat beading his brow (central air decades to follow)

his Ford Falcon station wagon,

his $800 dollar a month paycheck, his elation

granted an extra week vacation after forty years
glued to a lathe at the Lockheed Aeronautics Division
in Burbank, California.
A trip to the ocean, a picnic in the park, Yosemite in the summer,
Christmas tree shopping in winter, life's simple pleasures,
middle-class ecstasy to a nuclear family of five.

I think of the mother who scoured the newspaper for coupons,
the delusional uncle who dreamed of conquering Hollywood
with a shoeshine and a smile.

IV

A shoeshine and a smile: canvassing doorsteps,
dialing for dollars, the "anyone can get rich" infomercial…
Three million people spread out over 500 square miles.
A hunger so vast and shrill you can hear its echo
in your sleep, every morning on your way to work:
signs blaring sex in toothpaste, exotic getaways,
happiness in the hereafter.
And when you arrive safely at home:
the real estate agent at the door, the insurance salesman on the phone.
The doorbell at dinner when Dad and Mom and sis and brother
are seated securely at the table, Dad rushing to the door
to be greeted by a sallow faced Jehovah's Witness,
all of us knowing full well our souls not to be salvaged

when pork chops and gravy remain unattended
and Dad's empty chair waiting for a door
to slam in the face of God.

V

The face of God in so many aberrations:
Bible-toting evangelists, Islamic mosques, Jewish temples,
immense Catholic cathedrals, a Mormon fixture
like a gigantic mausoleum epic in proportion.

It's 1923, Aimee McPherson
gestures her sleight-of-hand miracles
to trumpet L.A. as the New Jerusalem,
the whole country lined up like starving hordes
at a banquet buffet.
Fruit growers, miners, wildcatters, farmers,
itinerant laborers, Slavic Jews with Irish names,
pariah parades on silver and gold steeds
grasping at rings a hair's breadth in reach,
while migrating enclaves of grifters & speculates
set the course for its inevitable future.
The Machine was the promise the Modern World awaited
and the black blood of L.A., Mid-Wilshire crude,
would feed the jaws that would devour its deserts.
The Machine was the promise, God the redeemer

and the thick black ooze of oil too plentiful
for a world hungry for the energy of fire.
The legacy of oilmen, land barons, religious hucksters
still riddle the terrain:
Herbert Eaton, C.B. Sims, Huntington, McPherson,
Hancock, Wilcox, Griffith, Doheny…

It's 1953, a Midwest family careening westward,
grinded gears on a rented six-wheeler,
my father's eyes frozen
on a memory of a war-time promise
to join the huddled masses
along palm-lined shores of the California coast.
Cleveland born, bred in a cold climate,
we of the eastern edge and Midwest tradition,
failing in faith of the Old World order,
lacking the legacy that could lift us from the grind,
saw in the green glow of the cathode ray tube
swimming pools and backyard barbecues,
shark-finned cars the size of cabin cruisers,
Want-Ads as thick as a telephone book
and a cloudless sky spangled with stars
and a sun-like God peering down
from the heavens.

Welsh on my father's side,
Irish on my mother's,
my Celtic blood alien to this singeing sun,

this ubiquitous brazen sky,

content, instead, with the harsh autumn wind

or occasional downpour

that saves us the fate of the more distant

Saharan sands.

It paints such pretty pictures, amigo.

To Latin neighbors the perennial promise,

to eastern eyes a postcard delight.

To a young impressionable eye

it's intrigue in dark alleys and whore houses,

a Hockney canvas,

the grit and grime of black & white lenses,

palm trees aglow in a summer sun.

Everywhere bronze-colored beach bodies

with sun-streaked hair,

dimpled bottoms and buoyant breasts,

half-naked men on surfboards or lifeguard towers,

the contrast of valleys and mountains,

outdoor promenades and hilltop retreats,

dreams manufactured in celluloid splendor,

cinematic gods and goddesses

spit from the volcanic kingdom of studio sets

and television screens,

gigantic slick fluorescent billboards

and phallic-shaped sports cars,

a downtown skyline piercing the smog-filled skies,

Parisian cafes, Swiss bakeries, English taverns,

Irish pubs, Mexican cantinas
scattered across the landscape
like exhibits in an amusement park…
And that time in '57 when the Dodgers came to town
and the L.A. Housing Authority,
under the guise of "imminent domain", displaced hundreds,
to build a sporting stadium in Chavez Ravine.
And no one seemed to notice nor care.
Newspaper images of armed police and bulldozers,
whole neighborhoods leveled and erased.
But after all, these were the bottom feeders,
the poor and underachievers, none of whom who could speak
a single word of English.

VI

No single word of English could suffice
to sum up the velocity of change that overtook
the lives of those of us, transplants from distant dwellings,
who found solace in sunshine and the exhilaration of escape.
All that we remember, all that can be contained
rekindles itself in scrapbooks and postcards
and cinematic memories.
Recollections of early fifties:
an era of aerospace and drive-in movies,
three children parents and a car in every garage;

housing tracts with bright plastic flags
proclaiming the birth of the San Fernando Suburb
and television screens glowing
through every tract home window
like beacons in the desert skies.

From this nucleus of being,
this heart in the center of Eisenhower America,
the world became real to me
in its Teflon-coated, crew-cut molded
Atomic Age illusion,
in its unreal, illusory, safe suburban shell.
The world became real to me
in corn-flakes and T.V. dinners,
in the eerie, echoing sirens of a fall-out drill.

VII

Sirens and fall-out drills. Every third Friday of the month.
"The missile silos and aerospace factories," my father explained.
"The Russians have us in their sights."
No matter how routine it seemed, I had to think hard
and keep my mental calendar on track.
What does a child of eight know of such things.
A sound so searing for so many years that I can still hear
that monotone moan echoing over and over

in all those nightmare nights.

Masses of boot-stomping armies,

little balding fat men pounding their shoes on tables,

bearded cigar-puffing Cubans in battle fatigues,

hordes of Chinese waving bright red banners...

Everywhere outside and around me a world drowning in despair.

To this day, I swear, I can still hear those sirens,

still see those faces, still hear those voices.

VIII

Oh, Lana Turner, we love you, get up.
                                    —Frank O'Hara

I can still hear those voices,

still see those faces...

What is it about these larger-than-life faces and voices

that embrace our minds on theatre screens?

I suppose there are worse ways to compensate

for the monotony of our lives.

For me it was Gable and Coop and Cagney

—Bogie to surface later on.

For me it was that take-charge demeanor,

testosterone on speed, the-way-they-had-their-way

with whomever or whatever was needed.

No internal struggles, no hidden voice asking

What is my motivation?

It was Rhett Butler matching wits

with that bitch of a Belle
or Gary Cooper staring into the face of death
with a quiet and calm resolve.

Or when the family gathered at the East Valley home
of an actress known for exceptional endowments
and a penchant for Pentecostal worship.
I sat next to a blond leading-man
in those 60s boy-girl comedies, finger picking
a six-string Martin,
everyone joining in, Sunday revival style,
for a sing-along:
Glory to the Master, glory to His throng
My Lord and Savior beside me,
His words and prayers to guide me,
His words and prayers my song.
Then to be introduced to the actress herself
looking nothing like the voluptuous siren
that challenged the censorship of the 40s.

Or that sunny day on the sidewalk,
a child of twelve at a traffic stop
to view a middle-age Lana Turner
blond hair clasped and pulled back,
Ray Ban shades, a convertible Cadillac.
The somber red light's ascent to green,
the accelerating descent into memory's vaulted distances…

IX

The accelerating descent into memory's vaulted distances…
The world itself descending into sleep, a sleep
that keeps us craving for what is false or what is real.
First it's fairy dust & cartoon kisses
then it's sultry vixens followed by
a sudden sense of loss, neither real or imagined.

When we went to visit his grave,
tucked neatly away beside a marble mausoleum,
we were surprised by the subtlety of the place.
For someone who took such pride
in redolent imaginings and grandiose dreams,
to be laid to rest in a simple garden tract,
a bronze plaque its only ornament…

Still, the high hillside, the English chapels,
the nobility of his somnolent neighbors…
If Jung was right and the collective unconscious
is the root of all mythologies,
and our mythologies breathe meaning
to what appears meaningless and mundane
then what better explanation for Uncle Walt, the eternal Pan,
piping melodies to immortalize our childhood?.

I was seven when the Magic Kingdom was little more

than an hour's drive from the highway.
A summer pilgrimage to continue till puberty.
Yet myths seem of less appeal when covered
in plaster & drywall.
Perhaps more was required, something of substance,
something more tangible and savory.

Enter the Heffner House (I was now thirty),
Granite and leaded glass, hillside views,
a private zoo, an Olympic-size pool and grotto.
And Disney's Tinker Bell inspiration, nude Marilyn,
that would herald a Hedonist Empire.

Arriving at noon for a political fundraiser,
my eyes focused on two topless nymphs
rising from the cavernous pool.
"Heff", in his usual attire of robe and slippers suggesting
we all join in for a leisurely swim.
A topless woman approaches me and offers to read my palm.
Another offers a line of coke.
I was cautioned by our host not to attempt
any physical contact.

In the evening a bevy of big-breasted blonds
sashay around the patio.
I sit near the edge of the pool, sharing a joint
with a beautiful red head.
We begin making out to the tune of Marvin Gaye

singing something about sexual healing:

And when I get that feeling

I want sexual healing

Sexual healing, oh baby

Makes me feel so fine

Helps to relieve my mind

Sexual healing baby, is good for me

Sexual healing is something that's good for me.

Suddenly a tap on the shoulder,

a voice reminding me the prerequisite

that guests refrain from physical contact with the bunnies

and there was Uncle Walt in his Tinker Bell Heaven

leering through the capacious clouds,

wagging his finger like a scornful father.

X

Uncle Walt and his cartoon heaven…

Those forgotten days of childhood in the 50s…

I recall how cheerful and shiny the whole world seemed.

Winters warm enough for play, summers beaming

with palm trees and ocean breezes,

spring and autumn were picnics in the park,

Sundays were solemn, reserved solely for worship,

Mondays to Fridays classrooms and school lunches,

Saturdays at the Drive-In for comedies and romances.
And the radio always blaring Bobby Darin or Martin Denny
And my mother in the kitchen or on the piano
And my father at his work bench
And my sister with her dollhouse and her dolls
And my brother doing handsprings in the yard…

How shiny and cheerful the world once seemed.
Everywhere you turned there was music in the air,
the scent of fresh cut lawns and orange blossoms.
Fall-out drills and warning sirens did little to disrupt the flow.
Middle Class Working America was alive and thriving.

How shiny and cheerful the whole world seemed:
mother & father, sister & brother,
the equivalent of all things good, all things safe and healthy
like white bread and peanut butter sandwiches.

XI

White bread and peanut butter sandwiches,
a mother, a father, an older brother,
a younger sister, a warm desert sun,
a suburban canvas fading from sight
and I find myself here, alone, ten office stories up

staring out the window,

sun on glass, memory hanging in the air

like a neon-flashing sign.

Thirty years since I began this poem,

Thirty years since my father's passing.

Father, in your khaki-colored work clothes,

your metal lunch pale and thermos.

You lived your life like a scratched record,

repeating itself over and over again.

Did you ever think this is where your life would lead you?

That dormant skill with paint and pen

that helped hone you a wife in a night class

on commercial art and drawing?

My duty-driven father,

a young Welshman with his estranged mother

on an ocean liner bound for the New World.

And when the news arrived, after such a short time,

of your own father's demise, a crumpled old pickup truck

on a highway somewhere near Buffalo.

At fifteen you were forced to face the mortality of souls

so a world at war seemed natural and unthreatening,

an easy ticket for instant naturalization.

And, at war's end, when the news arrived,

of an aerospace boom somewhere in Burbank, California

and veterans had an edge, you were quick

to make the journey, eager to shed those cold eastern skies

for a world of palm trees and perennial green valleys.

Now as I think back on that face,

me here in the heart of your newly adopted city,

you on that slab in that cold and empty space,

your eyelids forced closed, that gray pallor,

that cold, antiseptic morgue

where they laid your lifeless body.

No great knowledge lit your face.

No inner peace was present in those solemn-shut eyes.

No slight disturbance was noted

on the seismological charts.

The path of the stars remained unaltered.

No sudden storm clouds swept the sky with thunder.

Father, my fusion, this city's soil

now flowers in your flesh,

flowers and freezes where you lie, silent in your crypt,

in the low hanging hills of Hollywood.

It is only fitting, I guess,

that these hills should now claim you

as they have claimed many a wandering soul

lured by that hypnotic sign and the exotic palms

and that insatiable sun.

XII

That insatiable sun always counted on
to render such clear, detailed images in Kodacolor memories.
There's Bobby Torres with his Elvis snarl,
there's Bill Brown with his sister Donna
(though only ten, her breasts a teasing taste of womanhood),
There's Randy Tully with a pack of Lucky Strikes
tucked within his T-Shirt sleeve,
there's Betty-Lou, our teenage Muse, with her long legs
and strawberry blond curls.
There they all are and there I stand in the middle,
age 10, always the ham, always seeking the spotlight.
There they all are:
four ten year olds with my teenage muse
surrounded by fresh mown lawns, shark-finned Chevys,
suburban cookie-cutter homes,
a world untouched, impervious,
to the impending threats of A-Bombs and Castro's Cuba.

My father's vintage Kodak with its pop-out lens
could capture a scene as vivid and clear
as any elaborate Nikon or Cannon.
My immigrant father,
so totally sold on the American Dream,
wasting no time on leisure or trivial matters
constrained by a blue collar and a sixth grade education.

I picture him always at the work bench,

eager to supplement his meager existence,

pitching hand tools and mower blade sharpening

to friends & neighbors,

bending and welding and drilling till late hours into darkness.

My immigrant Welsh father asking nothing of life

but to care for and provide,

to keep constant a life full of perpetual promise.

XIII

A life full of perpetual promise…

That elusive and voracious American Dream:

There's no running away from it.

It follows you wherever you turn,

on theatre screens, on street signs,

up and down avenues, on park benches and bus stops,

on car bumpers and T.V. monitors:

that house in the suburbs,

that two-car garage, a Piggly Wiggly on every corner,

the neighborhood church waiting to greet you each Sunday

and for those who have found their way

to the top of the perennial ladder, the house on the hill,

the cool blue glow of chlorine

in swimming pool splendor.

I think of my father waking each morning to perpetuate that dream:

Hours on the freeway, in the factory by seven, coffee and cigarettes,

quotas and assembly lines, a paycheck at the end of the week—
nothing short of Nirvana to Depression-starved patriarchs.
It was the working world of men, welders and riveters, machinists,
lathe operators, airplane wings, hydraulic lifters, threaded pipes
household fixtures, thirty minute lunch breaks,
that end-of-the day beer with a friend at the nearby diner.
Nothing short of Nirvana for an immigrant Welshman
lacking credentials or a high school diploma.
Fish on Fridays, spaghetti -and-meatballs on Saturdays,
steak-and kidney pie every Wednesday.
How comforting it all seemed, how predictable and certain
seemed our lives.

XIV

Predictable and certain:
nothing short of misery in a teenager's eyes.
And those hot summer high school nights
cruising up and down the boulevards:
that animal ache, that insatiable longing.
And father's stern and prescient warning:
Remember to keep your pecker in your pants.
But we were sixteen. All dewy fresh and firm.
French kissing in the park,
sneaking a feel in the back seat of father's Ford.
Christina, pubescently pure, pouty lips, almond eyes,

sharp pointed chin, narrow waist and happy hips,
tits like succulent flowers.

O we sang the body electric, Mr. Whitman,
Our currents blazing, our circuits singed.
Like a bloodhound sniffing the air,
the musk of that memory has never left me.
Like a junkie unable to tell the pure stuff from the bad,
I have gone through life both pursuer and pursued
caught within the snare of my own ambivalent clutches.

Even now, staring into the mirror of my middle years,
the hunger tempered, the appetite gorged
with the fat of that fervor,
I am yet haunted by a demon wind,
a breeze blowing out from my youth
urging me follow the hot fragrance, renew the old fury,
succumb to the savor of that endless pursuit.

XV

The savor of that endless pursuit, the need to find yourself
through the words and actions of others.

The drama coach coughed and turned her head,
then lit another cigarette.

"Stop pretending," she shouted, "Be this boy Danny,
see into his eyes, feel his anger, suffer his anguish."
I gripped the knife firmly, moved slowly towards the front of the stage.
Was it all that simple? I thought. Remove the self that was me,
become the self that was someone else, someone, a fiction,
created by a someone else's dream?
I held the knife firmly at my side, imagined the blade
breaking through skin,
imagined a sense of fury in my blood,
a sense of heightened release.
But I was only sixteen, had always abhorred violence,
and suddenly I found myself conjuring up a darkness
I had never gone down before.
"Think," she said, "You have always been so careful.
Now you've been discovered. Do you act? No.
It's the inaction that creates the tension of the scene."
Strange how, thinking back on a scene
when acting seemed my only passion
I now look to find what bearing all this brings to me,
how a simple act of make-believe can widen our minds
and keeps us anchored on a floundering foundation.

XVI

On a floundering foundation, a city which percolates
within a galvanized grip of its overcrowded streets.

When the fires first broke out no one seemed terribly concerned.

After all this was South Central, far and away from any semblance

of reality in our iron-clad suburban shelters.

That a black neighborhood was up in arms over white police

seemed a common occurrence to what my Irish-American mother

referred to as the Negro's natural state of savagery and homicidal behavior.

And as the fires spread to Detroit, Cleveland, Chicago, San Francisco

we felt more and more insulated, more and more separated

not by our humanity, not by a sense of culture

but by the simple texture of hair,

the color and shade of dermatological fiber.

How could we reconcile these distinctions?

These were not people I knew,

these were Olympic gods or human gazelles

on cinder tracks or football fields.

These were frightening dark faces on Post Office Walls

or angry mobs burning down houses.

.

In my neighborhood people of color

were alien, antagonistic.

Our only contact, our only link

to these faceless abstractions

were viewed on urban streets, black-and-white scenes

involving snarling dogs and fire hoses.

Although music or football might, at times,

temper the fear, neutralize the hatred,

it would be years before some semblance of civility

would instill a more tolerant society.

XVII

A more tolerant and accepting society…

When Sal Mineo lit a "reefer" in the *The Gene Krupa Story*,
I was ten and knew only the evils of smoke
blown from the tip of a cigarette.
It was bad enough to sneak a puff
behind the Bowling Alley after school,
but a Lucky Strike was no reefer
and the smoke from a joint was no cigarette.
In my mind something sinister was at play,
something that led you down strange dark hallways
where harpies and demons lay in wait and
from a deep sinking well there was no escaping.

For these were the days of Sandra Dee on a surfboard,
Rock Hudson was straight and the *Doors of Perception*
was just a passage in a poem by William Blake.

These were the days before Huxley and Leary,
before the days at the Drive-In with Eleanor Ross
demonstrating the proper ways to roll a doobie.

Years pass and the stigma of intoxication.
melt away like so many other burnout restraints.
No harpies, no demons. Only sweet soothing embers
circling the stolid air.

"Feel," she said as she licked her lips
and placed her body above me—
the thick air of cannabis blearing the eyes
and fogging the windows.

Big, surly, curvaceous Eleanor Ross:
she could swallow up a whole crew of sailors
with what she held between those monstrous thighs.
Harpies and demons…
But this was L.A. in the late 60s: getting high
& humping in drive-ins . This is what we did,
sixteen and home-free and horny.

XVIII

Sixteen and home-free and horny…
Los Angeles and the late '60s:
Friday night on the Strip
looking for an easy lay,
high school girls with fake I.D.'s,
cruising studs and cops enforcing curfew,

smoldering flesh in tight jeans and leather,

drugs trading hands on every corner,

disgust with everything orthodox and accepted.

We stood in line at the Whiskey

to witness Jim Morrison or any fresh new

long-haired Svengali.

The West Hollywood Sheriff's Division

making random searches and arrests of anyone

deemed suspicious of random acts of pleasure.

I remember the night of the "crackdown",

the night Stephen Stills turned a song into

a teenage anthem.

A night sis and I got our first inside peek

of a holding cell with our disgruntled father posting bail.

A summer afternoon my friends and I were bounced

from a diner as management reserved the right

to refuse service to Beatniks and Hippies.

There we were: a generation caught in the starry dynamo of change:

long hair, suede boots, faded work shirts and jeans,

roach clips and hash pipes, condoms and birth control pills,

Lou Reed hipsters with the all girls singing

Doo dee-doo dee-doo dee-doo

and Jim Morrison inciting Charlene Peterson

to light my fire.

There we were: dancing to the tune of outrage and contempt,

our murdered Prince, our Camelot in ashes,

death sentences in Draft Cards...

And the Black Man always viewed as something alien,

suddenly turned Christ-like,

cacophonies of saxophone sufferings,

agony and anguish climbing the skies,

the cries of Ray Charles and Charlie Parker

scat-chanting a solitary sadness.

A reckoning was at hand,

a long, bitter journey for a suburban boy

bred on white bread and Jesus.

A harsh cold reality had splashed a visionary unguent in my eyes.

Suddenly it all came into focus:

Words like racism, bigotry, intolerance...

There we were, fists clenched, defiant, disillusioned,

longing for something, anything to energize the anger,

euthanize the anguish.

XIX

Longing for something to euthanize the anguish,

I was a freshman in college,

professors had gained the status of celebrity.

Students stood in line for hours

to gain admittance to a class

on "Psychology and the Therapy of Meditation"

—The ladies entertaining dreams of seduction,

ranking the virility of the male faculty,

comparing penis sizes and personal fetishes.

D. Metzger shocked the local Board of Trustees

by "sucking the cock of Christ".

I wonder what became of Doc Carson

("Wild Bill" the girls called him)

Leaning on the podium, casually dressed,

casually addressing the class

on the merits of Whitman and Thoreau,

the long-stem pipe gripped between his teeth

filling the classroom air with the scent

of Cavendish and Oriental tobaccos.

We set the "College Handbook of English Grammar"

ablaze with indignation.

We kept journals, undisciplined and raw.

"Honesty!" he would shout, "Faithfulness to detail".

And I the star pupil, the prodigal poet

detailing my distaste for everything

and anything deemed conventional.

Whatever became of that tiny office

relegated to a quiet corner outside the Department's

second-floor tower?

To one side: A neat and orderly exhibit

of Eighteenth Century artifacts and leather-bound books,

to the other: Books and papers scattered across the floor

in a kind of stream-of-consciousness disorder.

Race track results lay crumpled beneath a table,

a poster of Little Richard stared down from a wall next to Poe,

an old Smith-Corona gathered dust
where he hacked out pornography on the side
to pay child-support to an ex-wife
practicing E.S.T. in Big Sur, California.

They are an anachronism now,
These flagrant, flamboyant men and women of letters
—Their superstar status overshadowed
by an incessant urge for an internet startup,
twitters and tweets,
a cloud of gigabytes for hypertext horizons.

I wonder what became of the causes?
The current of energy that streamed through our veins,
the social evils ignored or neatly tucked away,
the hungry and the dispossessed lying dormant
beneath the ambient snores of middle-class America.
And all the while the Chorus of Authority
rang tired and torn in the tear-gas covered skies:
"This demonstration has been declared
An unlawful assembly! You are hereby ordered
To disperse immediately or be subject to arrest!"

The greater the odds the more steadfast our resolve.
We fought on every front: Imperialism, Racism. Poverty.
We organized, signed petitions, placed names and measures
on ballots.

Social and Sexual Injustice were the enemies.
We stopped a war, forced a President out of office,
won acceptance of alternative lives,
repudiated our Puritan past.

Now I sit and contemplate our triumphs,
forgotten by many, remembered by a few.

XX

Forgotten by many, remembered by a few,
it seems more than millenniums
this track of desert terrain
rose above its slumbering mountain borders,
a glow that circled our lives
and left our minds focused
on the pulsating lights and rhythms
inhabiting the horizon.
There was Pandora's Box on Sunset -
Fridays & Saturday nights -
Preston Epps finger-popping bongos -
Sky Saxon & The Seeds -
jazz solos at Shelly's Manne Hole on Cahuenga,
Coltrane, Miles, the Bill Evans Trio,
the speak-easy darkness of the Fifth Estate where the Beats
might gather to sample a poem or promote a new broadside.

But for me it would always be the acoustic simplicity
of the Ash Grove on Melrose:
Odetta teary-eyed, mournful, Big Mamma Thornton,
Mississippi John Hurt, Lightnin' Hopkins.
Names that conjure reverence and awe:
Tim Hardin, Hoyt Axton, Jim Kweskin, Phil Ochs,
Doc Watson, Tom Paxton, Dave Von Ronk, Bill Monroe,
the Byrds…
I dreamed you there last night, Sonny Terry,
that Hohner harmonica quivering like a train whistle
between those oscillating lips.
And there's Brownie McGhee (as always) beside you
foot stomping, finger picking that grizzly old Gibson.
How you made that little tin harp whimper and moan.
How Brownie kept pace to guide you and guard you
through that sightless tone and timbre.

Those hoots and hollers echo in my sleep.
I dreamed you still there in the corner,
in the dim lit darkness,
blood and bone reality hovering beside us,
spitting distance from where I dreamed you.
You, me, the Ash Grove on Melrose,
everyone and anyone alive and hip
in those magical days   in Hollywood   at night   in the 60s.

XXI

In the days back then we sat on the floor

next to the City Lights book rack

reading Patchen's *Love Poems* or Ginsberg's *Howl*.

No video games or personal computers.

With no internet,

college kids were known to read for recreation.

De Quincey's *Confessions of an English Opium Eater,*

The Teachings of Don Juan by Carlos Castaneda,

Heinlein's *Stranger in a Strange Land,*

The Martian Chronicles by Bradbury,

Thoreau's *Walden*, Skinner's *Walden Two,*

Soul on Ice by Eldridge Cleaver,

Das Kapital by Marx & Engels.

There was Pickwick in the Valley Malls

and Wallach's Music City:

revolving book racks circled the carpeted tile,

Sound Booths made possible a preview of one's favorite troubadour.

Opposite the valley was Poppa Bach in Santa Monica

hosting poetry readings and a chapbook press,

Dutton's in Brentwood with its eclectic store clerks,

Brentano's in Beverly Hills where best-selling authors

gathered to market their wares.

It was the late 60s before the blockbuster action film,

before the cinema multiplex, before the *virtual reality* reality.

On weekends Wilshire art houses

offered random samplings of *New Wave Cinema*

Polanski, Godard, or Truffaut.

We marveled at all the sex, the full-frontal nudity.

The silences, the stark shadows and dark themes.

We were ready.

The night when Kesey came to town with his Merry Pranksters

dispensing psychic flurries in sugar cubes and Dixie cups.

We were ready.

The four of us, byproducts of a working-class, blue-collar world.

We were ready.

Blue-eyed Randy, tall and gangly.

Pretty boy Mace, with his Buddha smile.

Tom, with his Hoosier's grin, sturdy farm stock,

and me, the long-haired wrath of all the mothers.

We were ready.

The Love-Ins, the Sit-Ins, delicious doses of dopamine,

diving naked into waterholes of enchantment.

We were ready.

Then Manson appeared and Kent State

and Nixon's crusade against free thought and dissent.

Hair cuts and full time jobs become the new order of the day.

XXII

Hair cuts and full time jobs:
parking cars at private parties,
filling bleach bottles at a food factory,
cleaning toilets and washing windows,
minimum wage and manual labor.
The summer of '69 when the Beatles split,
Manson went on trial, and
Weathermen were bombing buildings.
We found our lives adrift on a wave with
little or no wind at our sails.
Fear thick as flies followed our every move.
Fear of the Draft, fear of death, fear of a future
tied up in lottery numbers, student deferments,
2.0 GPA' s and a band of bureaucrats intent
on our self immolation.
There we were lost and adrift on unfathomable fate,
fallen like Lucifer refusing the dictates of a didactic God.

"They started at once, and went about among the Lotus-Eaters"

Fearful, fallen, and forsaken.
All roads led to escape.
It was a time to seek shelter, time to find refuge,
time to meditate in silence, to medicate our minds
All roads led to Laurel Canyon.

Laurel Canyon: as synonymous to the '60s
as love beads and peyote buttons,
as Peter Max and Sergeant Peppers Lonely Hearts Club Band.
Laurel Canyon: that stretch of mountains separating L.A.'s neon nights
and the shopping mall landscape of the San Fernando Valley.

It was winter. 1970, A night at Bill and Nicole's.
7800 Woodrow Wilson Drive.
The coyotes howled in the hills,
feasting on a neighbor's cat or a stray raccoon.
The Jefferson Airplane played endless on the phonograph.
We sat on the rug cross-legged and bare:
Nicole, with her long ringleted hair
and abundant breasts,
Bill Kennedy meticulously rolling a joint
between four nimble fingers,
my girlfriend and I smiling anxiously,
the dog on the sofa sleepy-eyed and drowsing.

A prism of colors glowed from a single candle
where we sat in a circle naked and sexless.
Words were incomprehensible.
Time felt fixed and frozen in the stars.

A winter night at Bill and Nicole's.
A tab of Acid swimming in a frothy cup of tea.
A night the moon came crashing through the window
like a giant steel ball and the stars lit up the sky like the Fourth of July.

XXIII

The stars lit up the sky
on the central coast at night, alone, 1972,
on a deserted highway, an autumn sky
littered with sequins and diamonds.
My eyes kept vigil
on the long stretch of 101 winding its way
through hillsides and mountain peaks,
winding its way through sleepy towns
like Atascadero, Templeton, and Santa Margarita,
returning from the kind of fare
any cab driver would kill for.
San Luis Obispo, my targeted destination,
a small college town in pursuit of an academic wakening.
It was a formidable feat: cabbing the midnight hours.
Jobs were far from plenty and school loans covered
a mere modicum of costs.
One did what one must to survive.
And the graveyard shift was especially brutal
to a twenty-two-year-old with classroom obligations.
But one did what one must to survive:
The all-night cab driver
relied upon for a pint of whisky
to a bed-ridden indigent
or an emergency blood bank delivery

or late-night chats with a lonely insomniac
at the diner.
The all-night cab driver
ignoring the dispatcher's numerous dispatches,
the flashing fare on the meter,
finding contentment in a shared nightcap
with a sultry blond intoxicant
retrieved from the local dive bar.

She called me "Hun". The booze on her breath
could peel wallpaper from walls.
She nearly swallowed me whole
before I found myself inside her
pounding away like a jackhammer mining for gold.
In the morning, I was greeted with a termination note
pinned to a twenty-dollar bill.
A month remained till winter break.
The worst time to be looking for a job.

XXIV

Winter break. A Central California College town.
A campus population diminished to dust.

Finding ourselves stranded in the after-wake:
Tom given a pass that year by parents
mindful of the Kentucky cold, Mace and Randy

no need to duplicate Thanksgiving obligations,

we remained equally intent to simply hang around town.

It was a desolate Monday morning.

The cold air had lifted.

We stepped out into the brisk morning sun,

the four of us, free from mid-terms and finals,

free from the scrutiny

of those who would determine our fates by a numeric sign.

Someone suggested a walk to the tracks.

The train traffic that morning was noiseless and still.

I can recall the excitement and exhilaration we felt

when the 9:35 arrived,

puffing and cranking into the rustic old depot.

The loud steamy hiss of the brakes and the shouts of the brakeman

a musical sonata to our ears.

We watched as the workmen performed their routine rituals.

We circled the train and the tracks, greeted the workmen and the crew.

We watched as the engine gathered steam to begin its northward journey.

A lone open box car caught the collective stare of our synchronized sights.

One by one we found ourselves rushing toward the dark opened doorway,

dragging our bodies over the hard wooden floorboard

as the train gathered momentum.

Someone found a stick of chalk and drew hopscotch on the wooden deck.

Using our car keys as markers, we hopped and jumped

along the rocking wooden floor,

while the clickety-clack of train wheels

kept rhythm with the slow descending night.
When, at last, the game could claim a victor
we retired to the edge of the car.
The scenery raced across our eyes: tree, grass,
rock, tree, tumbleweed, tree, cattle grazing, open meadows…
more trees, more cattle, more open meadows…
The panoramic landscape continued to chart the motion of the train:
Only the mountains remained fixed against the sky.

The Santa Fe and the Southern Pacific—Herculean steel and muscle,
gods of motion, smoke puffing vessels tunneling through the lines:
Atascadero, Templeton, Paso Robles, San Lucas, King City,
Soledad, Gonzales, Salinas, Castroville…

Speechless and reverent, we sat there on the edge of the car.
A world unknown and hidden from long stretch of highway
made familiar by our frequent commuter miles
rose up before our eyes in bright moon-dazzled mountains
and fields of flowers and grape vines.
Tom pulled a harmonica from pocket, Mace and Randy
broke into song, I kept time drum-tapping my knees.
There we were: four white boys channeling the likes of
Sonnyboy Williamson, Huddie Leadbetter,
Robert Johnson, and Howlin' Wolf.

Late evening and the engine came to a halt.
We found ourselves stranded at the Watsonville Station.
On the opposite track the Southbound coughed steam,

wheels squeaking, lurching forward,

signaling our eyes to seek another opened car.

Once safely aboard we steadied ourselves against the iron gated door.

"Time to head home," someone remarked.

We all assented with a nod as we looked out over the miles and miles

of artichokes and strawberries asleep in the glow of the winter moon.

XXV

A winter moon cascading a California sky.

A coastal hamlet wedged between mountain ranges

and infinite acres of farmland and grape vines.

We were up half the night sucking on a hash pipe,

swilling down six-packs of Colt 45.

George Middleton, a rare Business major,

in a school distinguished by future cattle breeders

and electrical engineers, was dependable for dope dealing

with a shrewd capacity to undercut all the local suppliers.

Tom, kept busy in the kitchen, baking and frying,

Randy fingering vinyl for Led Zeppelin,

Mace locked in the study, never comfortable

with the skunk-weed scent snaking the smoggy air.

And who could blame him? Rural college towns

hardly fertile ground for drug-addled hippies.

Jail time, suspension, revoked draft deferments

remained useful deterrents.

A rural college town. A college of farmers and technocrats.

Hardly a receptive venue for teenage refugees

from the Los Angeles suburbs, or misdirected architects

and malcontent poets.

XXVI

Malcontent poets.

The word got out.

The once abandoned voice of the California coast

had arrived at our cattle breeding campus.

Portraits and scenic displays neatly framed,

rare letter press editions and single page broadsides,

Ansel Adams photographs and family snapshots,

taxidermined eagles and hawks

highlighted the glass cased gallery walls

of our demure little library.

An evening of celebration followed:

a mesmerizing oration of a buckskin jacketed

defrocked Dominican monk.

At first I shared little interest, preferring Ginsberg

and the San Francisco Beats.

Yet the echo of that evening has never left me.

The ghost of that memory continues to haunt my dreams.

And the poet in question--my new found messiah,

my prophetic Virgil delivering me from

a personalised sense of hell.

How fitting it all now seems:

That same Central Coast where four closely linked friends

journeyed 200 miles to find learning and freedom
found themselves suddenly as one
with the Monterey Cypress, the coastal redwoods,
the white pristine sands at the foot of the Carmel River.
It would become, for me, the closest thing
to a religious conversion, an awakening of sorts,
and the Central California Coast a newly minted Mecca
to reclaim a world unspoiled, unblemished by humanity.
And here was a poet in the most classical sense of the word.
Robinson Jeffers.
No academic parasite living off grants and tax dollars,
no crowd pleasing Laureate.
Like Jeffers, it always seemed to me that writing
was less a vocational endeavor but more of a compulsion,
an unexplainable addiction to the rhythms and sounds
of language inherent in all that is perceived as beautiful.
It is the wonder of our world, the wonder and enchantment
that saves us from the sickness of the introverted mind.
What was always clear to Jeffers became clearer
and even more focused in my eyes.
In my own eyes now are always oceans and rivers, trees that climb
the dark slopes of the high sierras,
snow in the winter, red and gold orchards in the fall.
In my own eyes will always be the California coast of Robinson
Jeffers, the contrast of L.A.'s urban sprawl, its film noir,
its eternal summer sun.
In my own eyes will always be a world of words
to explain everything I am,
everything I was, everything I was destined to become.

XXVII

In my eyes are oceans and rivers, mountains and valleys,

beautiful nude models in oils and watercolors, the Graflex lenses

and sepia-toned visions of photographers and new-age cinema.

George Seferis, the Greek poet in his six-year journal wrote:

Sometimes it crosses my mind that the things I write are nothing more than

images that prisoners and sailors tattoo on their skin.

How do we determine what it really is,

what is worth the conveyance, what seems the most profound,

the less apparent.

The wholeness we look for and find in our solitude,

in the vast magnitude of what is seen, what is heard,

and what is worth sharing or revealing to escape the mundane.

We find music in whatever is there that can move us.

We sing to the world with our words, with our fingers, with our tongues.

In my mind the music of words should find their own structure,

adhere to their own unique sounds.

And now I digress.

For here I am writing this half-assed attempt at an epic.

And I get it. I don't have the celebrity of a Neruda or a Williams

or, for that matter, any of the great masters from Dante to Pound.

I don't know why any of this should matter.

Let's just call this a break in the program.

Feel free to go relieve yourself.

The Restrooms are down the hall.

—Begin again.
Haikus and sonnets. Villanelles, Sapphics, Odes or Sestinas,
Latin, Greek. and Asian devices. Old formulas from old voices,
old voices from dead mouths.
America has its own voice:
Saxophone riffs and blue notes from the street, Kerouac
with his stream of incantations, Ginsberg and Ferlinghetti.
Patchen with his dreamy prose and his Blake-like visions.
The choice is clear, the direction obvious:
To paint with a familiar canvas, to sing an unfamiliar song.

It is the process that defeats us in the end.
Recognition by consensus.
The merry-go-round workshops, retreats, literary journals, contests, prizes,
the reams and reams of magazine submissions…
How many subscriptions, how many donations
must we add to the cause, how many new directions must be sacrificed?

And those of us less inclined towards a teaching vocation,
less inclined toward esoteric study and academic chatter,
must content ourselves with a life more solid to the self,
a life less parasitic and controlling.

XXVIII

A life less parasitic and controlling…

The plan it seems is to continue to evolve,
let the memory unwind like the Janus myth facing forward,
while always looking back.
Those formative years, those pivotal moments
rising to the surface, bubbling in the brain
mining gold in undiscovered places.

How often each night I've dreamed of those days:
the four of us, teenage hipsters, suburban heretics
destined to defy each era's accepted cliches.
How does one account for friendships such as these?
The four of us, Valley boys, defiant, detached,
a formulated world laid out so certain, so safe.
We danced around all the demanding distractions
destined to teach us how not to think.
Joined at the hip in our discontent,
we reveled in the wrath
over haircuts and dress attire, school spirit
and refusing to salute the flag.
Grover Cleveland High's Boys VP,
struck an imposing figure lurking in the hallways,
always on alert for misfits such as we.

When war came and the Army recruiters,
Randy queried suggestions on effective ways
to avoid the Draft. The Recruiting Officer clenched his fist.
We all laughed and were summarily sent to Detention.

In college I joined Resistance,
Randy and Mace prayed for low lottery numbers and Tom ,
a Graduate scholar, relocated to Columbus Ohio.
Mace would remain in Central California selling cars,
recovering from a failed marriage.
Tom would land a top spot at a prominent design firm.
Randy would run off to deal drugs then find himself a wife
somewhere in Maryland.

It's now thirty years later, Tom prominent in his trade,
South of San Francisco, Mace on his second marriage,
running a business in Laguna.
And I, sitting here at my desk, the curser on the screen
blinking its yellow light , waiting for the words
to recover one more lost memory.
In between: father died; the war ended.
To this day we continue to count the dead…

XXIX

Counting the dead...

When young Phil Ferro, my brother's in-law, came home to us

that smoldering day in August, his tour of duty cut short,

his pinewood casket kept shut, we sat there at the grave site,

and gathered our thoughts.

Twenty year-old Phil Ferro, golden boy over 100 meters

of high hurdles, husband to high school sweetheart,

new father to new-born daughter, a rose marked page

in an American Tragedy.

And his young widow, six months shy of their second anniversary,

clutching the clenched hand of the grieving mother.

The mother, face swollen with tears, turning towards me

with: "He died so you could stay in school, grow your hair

and disgrace your country."

I don't think she was too happy with his sacrifice.

XXX

Sacrifice: the salve we use to ease the pain,

the lives we birth then bury in the bonds of

pride & patriotism.

But we survived, dear friend, we malcontents,

we defiant swimmers railing upstream

against the tide.

Your very name

Mace McCracken Morse:

Labials and sibilants rolling across

the alliterative tongue.

How many of us just felt honored

to be included in your company?

Always at ease with the world

and its inhabitants

yet secretly questioning everything,

sharing a fondness for rogues & iconoclasts.

The banner on your notebook proclaimed:

Rise Up Above the Tide of Conformity!

You had an edginess about you you concealed artfully.

Friendship flourished over Salinger, Whitman, & Thoreau.

You had a gift for gab an Irishman

would swear you chipped off a piece of the Blarney Stone.

When challenged to run for Class President

Randy and I stuffed the ballot box to guarantee you the honors.

High School Graduation seemed like a Fellini film

with you as the designated speaker.

Making friends came natural to you,

women were especially vulnerable.

In dreams I see myself walking up the steps

to the door of the house

I've returned to time and again.

That charming white bungalow surrounded by olive trees
and morning glory vines wrapped around an old wooden fence.
And you'll be sitting there as I always remember
in that second-hand easy chair
below a picturesque Whitman,
smiling through the filtered sunlight
like contented Buddha.

It is early spring, 1975,
the hardwood floor
makes that familiar squeak beneath your feet
as you rise to greet me.
There is never a need for handshakes or emotional embraces.
The air is always clear, the doors always unlocked.
The books are laid out,
a new snapshot has been added
to the memorabilia wall,
I observe a new painting or furniture piece,
comment on my discovery.
Perhaps Tom will be down from San Francisco
and Randy with his new girlfriend.

Later we'll gather round the kitchen table
over coffee and donuts,
discuss the local happenings in town,
maybe sample a recent poem or two…

Nostalgia is neurosis,

a Freudian once declared,

but I can still see the four of us,

set off against the coastal sunset,

journeying through the evening's twilight,

the air always clear, the doors always unlocked.

XXXI

The air clear, the doors unlocked,

I wander back to this place

I never seem to escape:

Los Angeles 1978, product of a working-class legacy,

reared on a love of language,

four years of Eliot and Pound, Rilke and Rimbaud.

Words on a decorative script declaring , "Bachelor"

of something. A proclamation

suggesting a proficiency in English,

a long held esteem of college breeding,

a challenge to someone less likely to fill cavities,

remove tumors or argue convincingly before a jury of peers.

Sweeping floors at 3AM, moonlight squinting

through the venetian blinds, a death-like quiet to quell

both bird and beast. The whole world asleep while I swept

away the hours at the West Valley Occupational Center.

A "real job", the lady at the desk explained,

with benefits and union wages.
Better than flipping burgers or washing cars I opined.
A step up from driving cabs or cleaning shit from dorms.

I grew tolerant with the night, took solace in the silence,
managed daily lunchbreaks of poetry and prose
beneath the cafeteria lights at three in the morning.

For me it helped to pass the time, offering a remnant
of something to be salvaged and held onto
for the sake of survival.

Over time I grew to see my life as distant and withdrawn.
Over time my world sank into darkening depths.
Vampire-like, I slept the daylight, woke with the night.
"So this is what you get with an English degree," my father would say,
remanding me to years better spent learning a skill, tackling a trade.
The girlfriend even more emphatic, likening me to a mule,
but mother imploring me to remember to dress warm.
The fact rent was paid, apartment furnished, seemed my only salvation.

A year had passed, days, weeks, debilitating hours.
My reading list was changed from *Poetry Monthly* to *Business Week*
and how to polish a resume.
I scoured the want-ads, heedless of pay, but intent on an office,
showered in daylight, where tool belts and key holsters were optional
not mandatory.

XXXII

Mandatory not optional: hours waking with the sun,
bright uterine walls and fluorescent ceilings,
IBM Word Processors,
insurance claims and actuarial calculations.
I welcomed the change.
A house in the Hollywood Hills:
stain glass views of oceans and evenings,
a prominent author as a next-door neighbor.

"Ah, so you're quite the well-read fellow after all!
And I suppose you felt, considering my celebrity
as an accomplished man of letters,
that I would share some sort of affinity
toward matters concerned with our illustrious literary heritage.
I must admit it is pleasing to discover such attributes
expressed so enthusiastically by one's new neighbor.
But really! All this talk about archetypes, myth,
and universal symbols is all a bit overdone, don't you think?
After all, what's to be gained from verses and epic novels?
The people don't read them. Who has the time?
what with the stress and pressures of modern-day existence?
Perhaps some college professor or some erudite dilettante...
And the Classics? Shakespeare and Homer and all that eloquent bunk...
Just a curiosity for someone trying to impress his friends."

Somehow I couldn't help but admire the veracity of his logic.

I listened and watched as a subdued ray of light
fingered a lead-laced window and lit an enormous library wall.
One could not help but wonder
at the shiny hardback leather covers, the How-To's,
and the flashy, sexy titles.
Indeed, he was one of those authors whose name stood out
and dwarfed the written bindings of each book.

I watched and listened.
I, in my overwhelmed humility,
a victim of middle-class necessity,
filing insurance claims and calculating costs,
gazing into this earthly paradise of leaded windows,
high arched ceilings and ornate wood crafted walls...

It was as if Virgil was tugging at my sleeve, directing
me away from my purgatorial existence.

XXXIII

A purgatorial existence...
We stare at the empty vessels on the mossy green waters.
Echo Park, forty years since my first arrival.
How did I find myself here after so many years

removed from this city's center?

Our family's first anchor

deep in the barrio, Highland Park & El Sereno.

The lotus flowers, once so prominent,

now only a fixture in the imaginary eye.

A rubber dingy sits abandoned, tethered to a splintered dock.

The bones of abandonment are everywhere.

The depth of the deepening air

drowns the senses, mollifies the simmering sun.

A lone Hispanic family of five

gather at a picnic table somewhere beneath a tree.

The sky's deep purple hovers above us, suggesting rain.

It is a strange and mournful day at the park,

a stone's throw from the downtown skyline.

Memories, like a Polaroid camera,

resurrect themselves and waken a distant dream.

I suddenly see myself

there in the water with my brother,

my father at the wheel,

the shiny white motorized boat drifting behind

a swarm of family fleets.

It is a picnic kind of Sunday.

Mothers and fathers gather with their children.

The skies are always sunny and never gray.

XXXIV

The skies are always sunny and never gray.

The yellow crocuses lift the light
from the San Gabriel Hills
and spot the green rolling mountains
with droplets of gold.
Every autumn I find myself here alone
among the peacocks and the herb-scented gardens.
The City's Arboretum, sixteen miles from the downtown basin,
remains the perfect retreat for a poet or a refugee
from life's harshest battles.

Gazing at the Queen Ann-styled manor
where Lucky Baldwin gave a dream life,
a pastoral playground to please a white-laced wife,
I think to a time of stiff-collared gentlemen and women
with parasols and bright summer dresses.
I think to a time of Model T Fords and transplanted Easterners
and farmers from the Mid-West
molding paradise in this valley of palm trees and eucalyptus.

A lake surrounds the house where we stand.
A Carriage House behind us in desperate need of repair.

Several swans and a gathering of geese approach the lake.

Mallards and Golden-Eyes slice the dark still waters with their bills.

What began as dream palaces to the likes of a Baldwin or a Huntington

now stand as remnants of a magical world,

a synergy of gardens, lakes, and flowers tax-payers and bond-holders

don't even know they've preserved.

XXXV

Upon the reopening of Angels Flight, the incline rail cars which ferried prominent citizens up and down the steep slope between Hill and Olive streets in the Bunker Hill district of downtown Los Angeles.

Resurrecting a past bond holders and tax payers

don't even know they've preserved...

How easy it seems to imagine those years

when streetcars once found favor over freeways,

when mothers and sons could cover long stretches of town

and still be home before supper.

Angel's Flight:

an ascendant funicular from Hill Street and 3rd ,

resting its wings on Olive

above the tunnel gates and the vehicular herds.

How difficult it seems to imagine those years,

time turning backward sepia-toned and faded.

The vanishing perspective of rails

that climbed near ninety and nowhere.

The Bradbury regal and resplendent

atop the tree-lined skyway.

And only a vague memory can recall

that one spring morning in April,

a mother and her son stepping into that angel-winged carriage

trudging the steep hillside,

hovering above a downtown skyline.

Everywhere a bright shiny canopy of sky, a yellow soothing sun

and white climbing towers.

XXXVI

Bright shining canopies and white climbing towers

hover above the long corridor of Sunset Blvd. at night.

Half-way down the track

you enter the doorway of the Seventh Veil,

the oldest strip club in L.A..

You are overwhelmed by a darkness

that blackens the very air you breathe.

A dancer emerges on stage,

a spotlight follows her every step.

There is something sinister

stirring in the dark.

A hulk of a human stands sentry

at the door.

A dancer, clothesless and shamelessly brazen
begins to gyrate and shimmy against a loud abrasive sound.
Her body mimics the motion of the sound.
The sound is harsh and numbing to the ears.
You can see Herod leering from his perch,
suds of stout dripping from his drooling tongue.
And the dancer your very own Salome
arched backward, spread-eagled on the stage.
Every twist, every turn threatens an invitation,
an unwanted intrusion we resist as best we can.
Light-beaming breasts, flexing flesh, sparkle of sweat,
a celebration of sense.
You can't help but think to yourself
how easy for some to feign passion and desire
when money becomes the only aphrodisiac
and you remain foolish enough to insist
her every move is reserved for your eyes only.
Suddenly you want to hold her,
overtake and absorb each molecule,
each atom of her existence.
You want to cling to her, wallow in her warmth,
swim in the sweat of her skin.
The man at the door looks on with a grin.

XXXVII

"I have the feeling that drinking is a form of suicide where you're allowed to return to life and begin all over the next day."
—Bukowski

The man at the door looks on with a grin

The songs of the sirens lure you
to the dark walls and beer-stained bunkers
of the businessman and all the lost spirits
who hide themselves among the dead.

Of all the watering holes of the world
—Harry's Bar in Venice, Les Deux Maggots of Paris,
The Bull & Finch of Boston, New York's Plaza Hotel—
L.A. is home to the "dive bar".
On every street corner, along every boulevard,
across a post office, a library, a church,
in the deep dark crevices of a windowless wall,
it incubates, waiting for the night to give it birth.

You enter from the workday, tired, withdrawn.
The whiskey welcomes you.
The whiskey, an amber lady swimming in a crystal pool,
welcomes you and winks her ice-cube eye.
Elbows and empty glasses rest on a shiny wooden mantel.
Darkness fills the room. A sense of loss and longing.

A pool table stands empty in the corner.
Two men argue over a game of darts.
The jukebox always sings nostalgic—
Sinatra, Bennett, or bluesy Ray Charles.

Leaning on a conversation that says nothing
and means even less, one voice after another
fills the barroom air with an emptiness
that echoes in a mirror
and weaves its way, face after face
reflected in the glass.
Why do we come here to lose ourselves,
to lose our world, our waking and sleeping alone,
waking and sleeping alone with something or someone
we can comfort, we can almost forget.
It's written in our eyes, in the face on the glass,
in the cigarette butts in a tray.

We must drink our fill of days, play Russian roulette
bottle after bottle,
until the days no longer matter,
and the nights are endless and lost.
So, we linger and we play, make deaf gestures of speech,
knock down a gin-and-tonic, a whisky sour
until the minutes begin to fade
and the moments no longer matter.

XXXVIII

The moments no longer matter.

It had been some time since I last saw Hank at the track.

It was one of those majestic autumns at Santa Anita.

A slight slivering chill bit through the tepid air.

The sky was a pale lapis blue, cirrus clouds skated above our heads.

I had just moved offices from downtown to Pasadena.

One of my colleagues had a horse running in the seventh race.

We were to meet at the Club House two floors up.

There was Hank at the bar where I always saw him

leaning across the counter, joking with a beautiful blond.

I sauntered over to say hi and offered to cover his tab.

He told me to fuck myself since he just put away his wallet.

He was looking much older than I last remembered.

Older and somewhat frail.

He asked who I liked in the Second.

I hadn't made my wager and said I was on my way

to join a diner upstairs..

He made a face and muttered something about hoity toity me

and why don't I save him a slice—"medium rare if you please".

I felt awkward and ill at ease. I assured him I was merely a guest

as membership was above my pay grade.

He started back to the bleachers with a slight wave of the hand

and a suggestion he'd meet me at the winning booths.

Two years had passed.

Al's Bar, 305 Hewitt Street downtown, March 14, 1994.

Hank has been dead four days now. A memorial service is underway.

Five or six punk bands headline the day's events.

A former lady friend, mother of his only child

is there to recite and share some personal reflections.

A riotous crowd overflows the bar and spills out into the street.

A chaos of deafening noise substituting as music rakes across the sky.

The crowd impervious to the fact that Hank preferred Dvorak

and Cèsar Franck.

I can almost hear him whisper from the grave:

"I'm glad I'm dead".

XXXVIX

Dead but never quite dying:

Days that fade and moments that never last.

But the city, the city remains.

The city and the world within the city.

The city half-imagined yet wholly real.

The city which dreams, which wakes and sleeps,

which dazzles the drowsy day.

This city. My city. Nuestra Senora Reina de los Angeles.

A city of infinite palms, cloudless skies, picturesque horizons.

A city that creeps, sleeps, dreams in perpetual motion…

And the night brings no respite to the hunger-heavy,

the homeless or the forever forsaken.

The night brings no rest to the workless weary,
the lonely, the lost, and the nearly forgotten.
The night is sleepless and unrelenting
from the all-night supermarket
to the twenty-four hour suicide hotline,
to the soothing radio voice
in the deaf, still hours of the embryonic morning.
The night is sleepless and unrelenting
and men sweat blood, tempting death
building an overpass on the freeway...
A store clerk is shot to death
defending a near-empty cash register,
a taxi-driver shares a cup of coffee with a hooker
at an all-night diner.
At the corner of Sunset and Vermont
three drunken blackmen wrestle on a park bench
over a half-empty bottle of beer...

In Los Angeles sleeping is a crime,
but dreams, dreams are what makes us who we are.
Dreams populate the landscape
and spill into our daily diet.
Stupefied and dazed,
we gaze into a world of forgetfulness,
a world of loss.
A world before desert casinos and mobster money
flittered away the shimmer and the shine.

XL

The shimmer and the shine.
A world once known for Hollywood parties,
fast cars, scenic highways, mountains of new money
no longer a credible guide to a travelogue promise.
But then came the new world order:
The rise of Japan and the Arab dynasties.
From these, perhaps, the future seemed certain.
For if cities have one common link, one saving grace
that transcends the dirt and grime,
it's the knack to remake itself, to recreate its luster and shine
with a new face, a new purpose creating new power.

The year is 1980:
My future no longer tethered to time clocks
or risk management procedures,
the time had come to focus my sights on material comforts
While I occupied my youth smoking dope, reading Kerouac,
cranking up the stereo to near deafness,
you studied Market Charts, risk assessments,
made high school valedictorian.
While I sat suspended from the Track Team
for refusing to cut my hair,
you were head yell leader, scholar bound
to Berkeley and Wharton.
While I drifted between jobs

driving cabs, cleaning toilets, underwriting insurance
you became the Money Maven Supreme,
the purveyor of less-than-investment-grade debt
and corporate raiding.

Valley boy made good,
you were an anomaly, anathema
to how money should be gambled or traded.
You resurrected a stagnant city
of low-life conmen and house flippers.
You were the catalyst for change.
And I was only too willing to hitch my fortunes to your wagon.
For one could not help but marvel
at the pomp & splendor of your Beverly Hills Empire.
You had the touch of Midas, the vision of a prophet,
a trading acumen that devoured the best and
biggest of the Fortune 500.

I remember the night on the elevator, working late,
you joined me on the descent to the lobby.
You grinned and gestured with your vapid brown eyes
as the elevator nestled us to the lobby:
"Have to put in the hours, you know.
Too many wasted on sleep.
Too many hours wasted on sleep."

I remember the day the SEC Auditors arrived and
you defiantly bolted the doors. A violation by all accounts.

As acting Manager I was summoned to notify the Home Office.

Multiple conference calls ensued. A compromise was found.

You were given till morning to put your house in order.

I thought to myself: this is what money is all about. Power.

Power to set your own terms. Power to levitate above the crowds.

It was some two years later indictments came down:

Insider Trading. Racketeering. A ten-year prison sentence.

You would serve a shortened term and return

many billion dollars richer.

And I…I would move on to less challenging dynamics.

My management years behind me.

XLI

My management years behind me.

The business of Money. Money as Business:

Stocks, bonds, mutual funds, annuities.

IRAs, 401Ks, 529s, Roth, Keogh, Revocable &

Irrevocable Trusts, Index of Leading Economic Indicators.

Ticker tapes, flashing symbols & illuminated digits.

Ten O'clock each Monday extolling the virtues

and rectitude of sound financial planning before

an over-lit studio set and an imposing array of immense

broadcast cameras and overhead television monitors.

Personal Investing—the name of this weekly exposition

proclaiming my first foray into Broadcast Glamour.

And the amplified voice from the telephone line querying:

How much higher do you think these markets can go?

or *How can I make more, lose less, and avoid all taxes?*

The return back to the office to tally the call-ins, the write-ins,

any and all prospects to fatten my future.

October 19, 1987: 9:59 AM. Camera 5 has the green light.

The countdown begins… 5…4…3…2…

Were on the air.

Below the monitors ticker-tape digits danced across the screen,

bouncing up and down in loud staccato clanks.

The numbers began to tumble, symbols turned red,

money bled, trillions reduced to billions, billions to a trickle…

The ninetieth day, the one o'clock hour—

Looking into cameras, beginning to stutter,

I asked myself in silence:

Is this the end, is this the grand finale we were warned about?

A retribution we suffer to atone for our avarice lives?

I tried tireless to remain on track, finger tracing each sentence,

each scripted word that could relieve me of my discomfort.

The business of Money. Money as business.

It all seemed so perfect to me. Self determination.

The sanctity of Work and Effort. It all seemed so perfect,

—those years of rebellion against the Capitalistic God a blur,

an impetuous jest.

But there I was captured in a million pixels in the past.

As I turned the page and looked up from the script
I muttered into the lens
something about wild rides and unpredictable fate.

XLII

Wild rides and unpredictable fate...

Earthquakes occupy this land, common as a cockroach,
as unpredictable as the weather.
You must always be prepared
the travel guides footnote with an air of nonchalance.
But to be woken from the early morning silence
with the rumbling, rippling
surface beneath you shattering windows,
cracking ceilings, tipping lamp stands,
triggering car alarms
is an event worthy of epic considerations.
We have not lived long enough
on this planet
to fully appreciate the implications
of such occurrences:
The subservience of man to the whims
and indiscretions of the elements.
We are a communal people,
arrogant and presumptuous,
comprised of various tribal origins,

united in our Judeo-Christian perception
of the world:
To multiply, prosper, and hold dominion
over land and beast.
We must seem comical to the eyes of nature,
comical and pathetically tragic.
But the sun continues to shine
its heavenly glow on this region
luring the Eastern Seaboard,
the unemployed Midwest,
the frozen habitants of the North,
the dark-skinned Latins to the South,
the Asians, the Arabs, the last remnants
of Europe's Communist Bloc...
And the builders and the speculators.

Earthquakes are common to this place,
earthquakes and mental disorders.

XLIII

Earthquakes and mental disorders...

To all who came to know him
Uncle George was a crazy man,
riding in make-believe parades
alongside Jesus, Julius Caesar,
and General MacArthur.

Mother said the war was to blame,
claims Roosevelt and Hitler
were his undoing.

As children, we knew him
as Uncle Bud the Comedian,
dressing in funny costumes,
teasing us with funny riddles
and limericks,
captivating us with stories
well past bedtime.
But later, after we were all tucked in,
snug within our innocence,
the curtain of illusion went up with a crash
and there was Uncle George in the living room
with Mom and Dad,
lashing out against the Communists,
the Jews in the White House,
the nigger-loving liberals…

His was a world of 1930 Black & White,
Busby Berkeley musicals, Valentino romance,
an Irishman's love of God and the Bottle.
He fought the Great War to make the world safe
for democracy and always questioned the loyalty
of anyone critical of our racist past.

The whole world may laugh at me

but let me tell you

I've seen them with my own eyes,

hovering in the early morning skies.

Not the saucer-like shapes

popularized by the movies.

Immense arrow-pointed wings

and metallic bodies that hide secretly

in the clouds.

It's all there in the Book of Revelation.

We call them "aliens" but they are, in fact,

agents of the Anti-Christ

and they are responsible for every disaster,

every upheaval we've encountered:

Wars, earthquakes, tornadoes, terrorist attacks.

Global warming? Don't make me laugh.

And this One World Utopia fantasized by the Left?

Devil-worshipping intellects, secretly sequestered

in underground caves of prominent universities:

Skull & Bones, Illuminati, Trilateral Commissions…

When I first took that shrapnel in my chest

during the D-Day invasion and they found me there

in that muddy ditch with Terry's severed arm

still clung tightly around my shoulder

(the poor bastard),

and I woke in that Base Hospital in France

I knew right then my life was spared

so I could return to the world to deliver God's message

and salvage what souls were left worthy of salvation.

Uncle George no longer lives in upstate California

with a widowed sister.

No longer builds Roman chariots in his spare time,

dreaming of Cecil B. De Mille productions

that will end all wars,

bring God back to Hollywood.

Ninety-nine years and a heavy urn of ashes

now reside in a National Cemetery in Riverside.

His only sibling, my mother, well into *her* 90th year,

insists the war was to blame,

claims Roosevelt and Hitler were his undoing.

XLIV

My mother well into her 90th year,

brushes oil on canvas

(Imitations of overlooked classics,

still lifes, the banality of provincial seascapes).

personable, petite, anxious to please,

easily hurt, fragile as a Japanese lantern.

In her younger years she taught herself piano.

Sunday mornings we woke to the chords of *Moonlight Sonata*

or a nocturne by Debussy or Liszt.

She took up opera , painting classes at night school.

The bookshelves were full: The New World Encyclopedia,

books of history, books of science, and an odd selection of poetry,

both sentimental and avant-garde.

A high school drop-out, a stay-at-home mom.

Though the spirits in her head might roll back her eyes

and bruise her tongue she persevered.

The neighbors thought her mad.

The one most relied on, when the spells surfaced,

when father was away,

slipping the tongue depressor in her mouth,

restraining her shakes and spasms

became her most ardent adversary,

the neighborhood Gestapo, suspicious of anyone

not in sync with the lemmings of Vanowen Avenue.

No one understood you.

The neighbor most relied on, Joyce Lewis,

ten years your junior, knew only wifely duties, raising

children, gathering gossip like pearls.

Music and painting and higher learning

was something reserved only for the privileged few,

the privileged few or the mentally disturbed.

But a good Christian woman from the South,

she took pity on your flaw and offered assistance

to my overworked father.

The seizures continued.

Then one day they vanished and were forgotten.

The neighbors, the church groups you envisioned
in all those Norman Rockwell designs
found you odd, too easily distracted by things
deemed mysterious and awkward—exotic dance music,
faraway India, sitars, tablas, and yoga,
Italian opera, Viennese waltzes…

After all, this was the 50s and my mother was no hippie
and New Age was a term unlikely to find its way
to English language lexicons.

You could never accept this world, mother,
the cold, bitter reality of its existential surface.
Your father deserted you for Irish Whisky and the horses.
At thirteen you were left to care for a younger brother
and an itinerant mother.
All the plans you made failed you:
the amiable ambitious husband,
the tight woven family, the ascent from poverty
to a state of high refinement.
You were so sure I would be your master work.
I would succeed where father had failed you.
You had painted over everybody else.
Father left us early, a weak heart and failed kidneys,

sister and brother rushed off to be on their own
while I hung on to finish college.

You were so sure I would be your master work.
The books, the acting classes, the private tutors.
When I mentioned moving upstate to further my studies
you made me promise to return as father was sickly and dying.
You hated being alone.

Everything around you now seems alien, ghost-like.
The castles in the clouds you built are weather-worn,
cracked with fissures of disappointment.
But you still make music and paint through the doubt, and I,
I will always remain your work in progress.

XLV

A work in progress
that's how I've always viewed myself.
I remain forever at odds with what,
in the Capitalist culture,
defines us by what we do.
Who we are and what we are
are abstract equations.
Mind and matter are extraneous fodder
to the functional machinery that defines our lives.

Thus I am what is commonly referred to,
by the lexicon of pedantic pencil-pushers,
a *sales executive*—the word *salesman*
sour to the tongues of my distinguished comrades.
So what is it we're afraid of:
The curse of Willie Loman?
that delusional dream of an honorable order of men
rising from the rubble of tarnished trophies,
gold watches, underfunded pension plans.
No, we are professionals:
vested suit, computerized intellect
inputting, impacting, programmed for any given
circumstance or objection.

Where do I fit in among all this?
With my reverence towards Blake
and early Twentieth Century Literature.
Where do I fit in among all this?
Trying to punch holes through a system
that rewards uniformity and casts a jaundiced eye
on matters outside the predictable, the redundant.
To abstain from all of this, to remove myself,
to refuse to assimilate while cocktails and conferences
highlight our weekly toll, infusing our minds
with intoxicants of sailing yachts, exotic getaways,
elaborate golf resorts, high-priced hookers,
and shiny new luxury cars.
Where do I fit in among all this?

Wasting my years genuflecting,

gesticulating to the fear, greed, and hunger

of the affluent upper classes.

Consider the alternatives:

The college professor in wrinkled suit

and disheveled manners

trying to keep ahead of the academic wheel,

tenure waved before his nose

like carrots to rabbits,

papers to grade, articles to publish.

And what of the sharp young lawyer?

The pride of every son's mother,

in and out of the courtrooms,

wracking up billing hours

with little regard to justice or human values.

Or what about the anal-retentive C.P.A.

organizing, tabulating each aspect of his life

in alphabetical, chronological, tax-deductible order?

And lest we forget the aristocrat physician

with his race horses and stock portfolios,

the pharmaceutical salesman's delight?

I grow old, I grow old,

I shall wear the ends of my condoms rolled.

I think of Keats' *negative capability* as I clutch

the set of keys to a new cream colored Mercedes:

the scintillating smell of Palomino leather,

the luster of gleaming metal…

In Lotus Land poets should get a job
or move to another planet.

XLVI

Summertime in Lotus Land
and the Hollywood Hills celebrate the hot-cool nights
with fireworks and music in the skies.
The days pulsate like a penis erect and aroused
and everywhere the crickets hum
like live-wire in the bushes.
A woman writes me from the tropics
reminding me the smog must be heavy
this time of year.
But today the air is clear.
From my second story balcony
above the Sunset Strip
I can see all the way out to the Pacific.
The clumps of skyscrapers
from the downtown district
to the picturesque palm trees
of Beverly Hills
I can imagine what my father must have felt
on his way to war in the islands
off the Guinea coast,
as his eyes first caught glimpse of this golden land,
the seductive lure that led to avow:

here was a world to build a future.

Old dreams die slow.
Police sirens echo
in the streets below.

XLVII

Police sirens and helicopter blades
hover above the Hollywood skyline.
Click the channel and there we are:
an incidental hardware store
on the corner of Beverly and La Brea.
The time is a little after two. The date: Summer 1985.
The eye of the sky looks down upon
four middle-aged shoppers, a store clerk, and a man
emerging from an idling car.
The sky is amazingly clear, swimming-pool blue,
bright and dazzling, cloudless and calm.
Approaching the Kitchenware Aisle, I am greeted
by a Latin-like voice and the glint of polished steel.
A young Hispanic face, pot-marked and pale,
 eyes wide as a cornered mouse, begins to shout:
"Don't say anything, don't look at me,
move to the back of the store," as the barrel of a 9mm Glock
digs a furrow in my wrinkled brow.

(Blood rushes in an icy torrent leaving the body fixed and frozen in fear. I suddenly see myself above the store looking down at the stage-like scene below. I see myself and five nondescript trance-induced victims led single file down a narrow hallway, into a tiny bathroom next to an exit door.)

I think to myself: so this is how it all ends for me:
In typical existential fashion, right out of a Camus novel.
I think to myself: so this was to be my life's final statement:
One of five ill-fated robbery victims facedown
on a blood-soaked bathroom floor
just in time for the 6 O'clock Evening News.
So this was to be my life's final exit from the stage,
the final act to a life of perpetual promise,
a life identified only by its limited successes
and the struggle for purpose and validation.
So this is how it all ends for me:
Not in a barroom, backward off a stool, like Lionel Johnson,
not in a hospital room surrounded by well-wishers,
not in the arms of a devoted back-street mistress
—the indignity, the humiliation of it all!
So this is how it all ends, I sighed dispassionately,
with one brief explosion to the brain.
What was and might have been…

(Reluctantly returning to my separated self, I watch as the diminutive man with the large metal wand lay plunder to the little vacant shop while a compliant crowd stood silently facing a sterile bathroom wall.)

Seconds crawled in silence.

A sound of the front door opening and closing.

Prolonged silence.

Finally the silence, itself,

made obvious the culmination of the crime.

A quick inventory check determined a $185 dollar shortfall,

the store clerk rushed to the entrance to insure no future intrusions.

The men all hugged and cradled their wallets,

(a bit of an oversight by our captor).

A middle-age woman made happy note of the jewelry she wore,

relieved and surprised at the oversight.

An elderly local from the nearby Hassidic neighborhood

uttered a stoic phrase of fatalistic resolve.

(A fifteen minute police report soon followed in a casual-yet-droll
and official manner.)

XLVIII

In a casual-yet-droll manner,

those inhabitants that frequent Canters Deli

in the Borsch Belt district of Fairfax and La Brea joyfully

noshing down their blintzes and bagels.

It's early Saturday morning.

The woman at the booth seated across from me

rivets her gestures against my bloodshot eyes.

I gaze unnoticed as her tongue slides from her upper lip

down to the deepest depths of my fastened mind.

With her right hand she brushes a strand of hair from her face.
With her left she pulls a small mirror from her purse.
Peering into glass, she rolls the red lipstick-tube methodically
along a puckered mouth.
Fingers like flowers glow into light.
The air is actualized only by her presence.
Everywhere fingers, lips and heavy-lidded eyes.
Everywhere long lacquered limbs, an English aquiline nose,
soft, slender torso and arms.
Everywhere hair of burnt umber glittered with gold.

Not enough can be said about these gestures of light
against a crowded dining room wall.
Not enough can be said in words what light and shadow alone
can radiate and refine.
Our eyes meet briefly.
She quickly turns away.
I measure and record each movement,
each frame or feature, the regal, the transcendent
on a plane far above this earthly terrain.
In the restroom I argue with the mirror
on approaches and endeavors.
I convince myself of the inevitable outcome
of such chance encounters.
I become a devotee of determinism, a willing participant
in God's Divine Plan.
When I return a man, tall and noticeably handsome,
slides into the booth beside her. She smiles; they kiss.

A sudden demon-like wind wipes her image
clean from my eyes.

XLIX

A demon-like wind is native to this city.
The *Santa Anas* we call it.
Zephyrus never knew a daughter more fierce.

Last night I heard the shutters
shake and rattle where your teeth bit
into the sleeping house.
Tree branches snapped and scraped
against the windows.
I could hear the moan of a haggard sailor
lost and abandoned on an empty isle.
I imagined the Banshee's cry, the screech of an owl,
the protracted howl of a hungry wolf.
A fierce desert wind, a mythical maelstrom
awesome and wild.
Dry-throated it tumbles through alleyways
like abandoned newspapers.
A palm frond skids past a child biking uphill.
The sky—not blue but scorched blank
like a parking lot after midnight.
This is L.A. exhaling its hot summer lungs.

Windows rattle not from ghosts—but from everything

left unsaid between neighbors.

No apology in the wind, only the smell

of citrus burning in the distance.

L

After days of relentless rain, Southern California is awaiting the most intense storm system
yet, with evacuations ordered, roads covered by water and mud, and residents anxiously
eyeing already saturated mountainsides denuded by wildfires.
—Associated Press,
December 10, 2010

Burnt citrus, grass gone muddy and brown,

eroded hillsides, inconvenient rain

on a city ill-suited for moisture.

The river rages along a narrow gorge.

Two drownings in less than an hour.

Not accustomed to the wet,

a teenager reaching for a fishing pole,

a boy of ten on his bicycle

      slipping on wet concrete…

Cars backed up for miles on the Angeles Crest Highway…

I move to the window and watch a blackened sky

rumble and shake, light flashing, a hard hitting hale

pounding the shingle roof.

It never rains in Los Angeles

        that's what they say

and that remains the mindset

of the three million plus that inhabit these hills and towns.

I cannot help but laugh at the poker-face weatherman

who insists the rain level remains insufficient

to offset the continuous drought.

Was that Noah I saw at the intersection today

directing a menagerie of chickens, goats, and cows?

LI

A menagerie of tank-top nymphets, roller-blading couples, men and women on bikes, leather-skinned bathers and children drenched in sea water form the current population along the Venice Boardwalk on a typical Sunday afternoon. I still can recall the time, thirty summers past, another Venice had welcomed my eyes. *Venice West* they called it: poets, musicians, street jugglers, out-of-work actors, war protestors, "devil-may-care men who have taken to railroading out of sheer lust of adventure". I had always known there was another world outside the quiet calm of the San Fernando Valley. And it remained a liberating experience when I ventured into the circus-like smells and kaleidoscopic colors along the Venice Beach boardwalk one afternoon in 1968. The aura of the Beat had made its way from the North Beach coffee bars of San Francisco to settle quite comfortably in this odd little aberration of elderly retirees and street vendors and bohemian artisans south of the manicured shores of Santa Monica. For here the Beat was king! The Beat was everywhere: in African conga rhythms, in the wild store-front windows of hand-painted bath tubs and gypsy fortune-tellers, in the head shops and incense-scented bookstores, and the jazz clubs and the semi-nude traffic that lined the sun-baked asphalt and the burning summer sand. Here the Beat was everything! For the Age of Aquarius, with all its Madison Avenue hype and distortion, was a comfortable light year away. Here the primitive dreams of Picasso and Gaugin had found a true-life vision. Here was the raw reality of human existence moving in step to the tribal rhythms of congas and sea-gulls and saxophones and children's voices and rotating gold-skinned bodies moving in sway with the ocean's ebb and flow.

LII

In sway with the ocean's ebb and flow
a river and the city it centers.

My city too has its river—masked
            and camouflaged
by a concrete embankment
the Army Corps of Engineers
                concocted
as retaliation
for the great floods of '38.
No Mississippi this river,
no New York on the Hudson
        this city.
Cold, gray concrete embankments

north from the Valley
running south through
the city's center.
Brown not blue this narrow waterway, brown
and weather-washed
from hillside runoff, intermittent rain.

We know your vast sequence,
silvered by sun on your rippling shoals,
know the narrow shorelines
and the high leaning levees.
We know you as we know
the dance and rhythm of the blood.
For you are the central source,
the main artery
that feeds and nurtures the city's heart.
You cradle our infant eyes, mother
our most infantile tears.

We dream you into being,
will your waters
across the wide Owens Valley,
land sifted green through
the deft Mulholland touch.
Where once stood sagebrush and cactus:
rose gardens and swimming pools,
oranges and apricots, pine trees and pomegranates.
Where once stood limestone and desert chaparral:

singing streams and reservoirs,
a mirage of tennis courts and putting greens,
palm trees swaying in the sweltering sun.

Flow, flow, flow,
you ancient river,
flow past my childhood
memories on horseback,
catfish fishing along your unpaved banks.
Forty years I've watched you
girdled and dammed and buried in granite.
Fifty years I've watched the world forget you,
forget your beauty, forget your past.
Fifty years and still counting…
Fifty more years to be remembered
your glory waters Pacifica!

LIII

Your glory waters, your harsh winter rain.
A sublime contradiction
what these ions leave behind:
Snow-frosted mountains
as noble as any Alpine horizon.
April like a morning peacock strutting
across the sparkling green hillsides,

canyons covered in flowers,

flowers adding color & fragrance

to this stark desert parchment.

All season long these waters

have saturated these dry adobe hills

to blush verdant and green

across the warm vernal sunrise.

It's been three years since my failed first marriage,

womanless, withdrawn from family, from friends.

For three years I've watched this aerial display

of blossom and birth unfold before the day-long sun

and the hot oppressive smog.

Each year the vibrant green sycamore, the proud stately oak,

the manzanita and the poppy,

the blackbird in the plum tree.

Each year the sweet fragrance of gardenias,

the yellow jasmine,

the symphony of bird song.

Each year I watch from my window

this bountiful display of music and magic and grandeur.

A sublime contradiction to these sad withered eyes,

this dry desert heart.

LIV

There is nothing, absolutely nothing,

To these sad withered eyes, this dry desert heart:

No flower, no tree, no snow-capped mountain,

No babbling brook, no river or stream,

No diamond, no pearl, no shiny sports car,

No gleaming mother-lode of gold,

No animal, no mineral, no exotic tropical isle,

No sunrise or moon shimmer,

No sacred sonnet or symphony,

No morning bird song,

No holy prayer or evening vespers,

No dance, no dream, no magical dimension

As beautiful, in this wandering world,

As a beautiful woman.

The long silk hair, the skin like satin,

The smooth, curvy legs, the rotating buttocks,

Those round and rosy breasts…

Here, they grow like weeds:

At every street corner, at every supermarket queue,

At every reception booth, at every turnstile and stand,

At every and all outstanding male fantasies.

There they are, staring down

From every theatre screen, every magazine counter,

Every topic and newspaper ad.

There they are

And here we continue to grovel

Like wide-eyed urchins

Staring at a storefront window of savory delights

And that unlikely prospect

That one of these celestial visions might

Like Newton's apple,

Fall freely and without hesitation

To the tired and blistered feet

Of this mere mortally grounded man.

LV

Of this mere mortally grounded man

daisies and dildos hum their electronic pulse

in my hunger heavy heart.

All year round this city teems with the heat of love

in pick-up bars and night-club dances,

in air-conditioned office suites,

behind locked doors in dingy motels,

in scenic drives atop the downtown view,

in fog-filled windows of parked automobiles.

This city steams and seethes with love.

Love perennial like dildos and daisies,

love unrequited, love unsuspected,

love unrelenting, love unfulfilled.

This city teems and steams and seethes with it.

The people when they sleep dream of it,

dream of sweat-dripping flesh,

the wet sheets and the piston-pounding rhythm.

They dream it and speak it and wear it on their bodies

like the musk of a fine perfume.

And love is conspicuously absent in this world.

Desire is everything.

Love without lawyers,

love without wills and trusts and marriage counselors,

love without toothpaste and deodorants and condoms,

love without Bibles and ministers and rabbis,

love without billboards and bumper stickers and "personals",

love without prenuptial agreements,

without fear and greed and false infatuation.

Love without daisies and dildos and all the frivolous

rituals and restraints.

Love without batteries to charge our depleted hearts.

Love without money or promises or lies.

Love is conspicuously absent in this world.

Desire is everything.

LVI

Desire is everything.

The streetcars are gone.
We make our way across the rain-soaked sidewalks
and find refuge in the doorway
of a downtown bar.
You knock down four sidecars,
I empty a half bottle of 12-year Scotch.

When the rain pauses
we make our way to a nearby hotel.
An old black woman with gnarly skin
peers out the window above our heads.

Our eyes mirror a wasteland desolation
of a city once viewed as a shimmering mirage
in the heart of the California desert.

You look to me as a savior, a guardian from gloom.
We make love in the stillness of solitude
and treasure what little we salvage
from an alcoholic binge.

LVII

Binges of alcohol to relieve a broken heart...

He was of all things, a gentleman.
A rare commodity in a land that measures refinement
by price tags and clothing labels.
Meticulous in dress and manners, scented with French colognes
and cigars from pre-embargo Cuba,
his sense of being was East Coast intellectual
tempered by a taste for the unconventional and irreverent.
Though many resented his links to his brother's fortune,
(stocks and bonds and a house above the glamorous Strip),
he remained cordial and kind
even to the most envious of enemies
in the stilted confines of the University's English Department.
Fame never found you, Robert,
the way fortune found your brother—
all those wonderful drawings and those sad, sarcastic poems...
You took private delight in the turbulent sixties
and questioned any and all resistant to change.

When asked for suggestive sayings for his brother's memorial,
I suggested W.C. Fields who'd rather be in Philadelphia.
He surprisingly acquiesced
to the more common "gentle good night".

When informed of his own demise,

and after shaking off the shock of this sudden revelation,

I was certain Robert, too, would find Philadelphia

a preferable diversion.

LVIII

Venice Beach, California, a preferable diversion

to the sterile façade of its neighboring Marina.

There I would find myself

at a literary retreat fostering some sort of Post Modern revival.

The featured reader, an East Coast poster child

of good taste & breeding, the darling of the Obscure and the Incoherent.

I approached, seeing an opportunity,

to avenge my own years of neglect and disaffiliation:

"Do you have any idea what it's like working a graveyard shift,

driving a taxi or cleaning toilets, setting traps for rodents,

washing windows, living on tuna fish and beer?

The Prep Schools, the Ivy League lemmings, the grants,

the fellowships, the Iowa Workshop Retreats…

The Real Poets, I mean the people who know real hardship,

real intellectual struggle: Whitman, Kerouac, Neruda

or Hank, that dirty old man…

No Xanax and Lithium to substitute for reality,

no stipends to keep your belly fed..."

Before I could finish, I noticed

a crowd had gathered and began pulling me away

from the disheveled speaker.

To be fair, I suspect Hank would have been far less intrusive,
and though I had pounded down six shots of Bushmills
and a pint or two of a frothy stout to make old W.C. proud,
still I would have been better served by a whimsical aphorism,
a disarming cant rather than the ranting rage that overcame me.

It's been some twenty years since that evening.
The victim of my verbal assault has returned
to promote his latest effort.
A line forms at the Book Store.
I join in for the ritualistic signing.
Life has been good to both of us.
Me with my banking career, you with your celebrity.
No need for public redress, no need to put things in order.
But I can't help but think everyone, poets included,
need a real job, a real stain of dirt beneath the nails.

LIX

Dirt beneath the nails, hardship, struggle.
Take it all away. Stock up on privilege, pride,
perennial comforts: what remains: ten milligrams
of Valium, Xanax, Zoloft, Oxycodone...
and you keep asking yourself:
why am I unhappy? Why do I feel empty?

Where is the God I was promised?

The City of Angels they call it. And it's all here

just like the photos in the travel guides:

The palm trees, the mountains, the lotus on the lake.

It's all here: the ubiquitous sun, the freeways to take you

to whatever heaven you need to ascend.

It's 8 O'clock on a Saturday morning. West bound on the 101.

Up half the night. Tequila shots and beer.

At 75 miles per hour and everyone seems to be passing by.

I feel like I'm on the Autobahn in Germany.

I ask myself: Where is everybody going? Eighty-five,

ninety miles an hour…Why the rush? Why the hurry?

Warning signs everywhere: SPEED LIMIT 65!

It's a weekend. The malls don't open till 10. The beaches are overcast.

There seems to be a madness in the air. Everyone intent on escape.

Everyone in a destination panic.

Have I missed something? Is there an asteroid on target?

Have the bad guys declared war?

No matter what the habitat, no matter what the status

everyone, everywhere in flight.

I think back to a time when I was six

and the family piled into the Ford station wagon

ready to give that sparkling new Hollywood Freeway a trial run.

The atmosphere was festive and exciting:

the shiny smooth asphalt reaching out toward the mountains,

the on-ramps and off-ramps like launching pads,

the trickle of automobiles like ants in a giant ant hive.

I was only six but even to those young and innocent eyes

something very special seemed clear.

Time, death's cruel tracker, mortality's constant reminder

had been dealt a blow from the wellspring of progress.

What took nearly half a day to travel from Valley

to ocean was now reduced to an hour.

Mom and dad grateful for any cost savings that could be garnered.

Time. Time the archnemesis of all we hold sacred.

Time that wears away the flesh, that taxes the mind,

that withers the flower.

Perhaps that's what lures us to these roads

in such rapid and brazen defiance.

It's not the speed limit postings. It's not the allure of adrenalin

or the velocity of motion. It's a gesture of disregard, a denial of time

and everything that can't be conquered.

LX

A denial of time…

Sirens whisper

     where the lotus withers.

The lily pond in the park gather moss,

     the water turns stagnant.

Peddle-boats and canoes drift aimlessly

where straw-hatted Casanovas strummed
their spoon-June-tunes
       under a platinum moon.
The streetcars are silent, the tall white stucco
       and the red-tile roofs
still shimmer against the bright orange sunset,
but the barefoot summer mornings of baseball
       and bicycles and old people
       feeding pigeons from benches
are ripples of light on a flicker of frames.
Ghosts of ruddy-cheeked children
and the laughter of young women
       wooed by young men
haunt the galleries of the air.
The city devours its youth the way Sirens
the shipwrecked and the home-hungry.
       And still they come:
the sun-worshippers, the war-weary, the broken-in-spirit
as the huddled hordes before them,
       as my father before me…
El Mexico made you a goddess,
proclaimed you queen of the angels,
       La ciudad de la reina de los ángeles,
christened your rivers, valleys, and mountains,
built temples and missions to worship you
— Only to watch your treasured Mecca
surfeited by Anglo intruders,
Yankee invaders from eastern waters.

Now look how we reward your loyal subjects:
	hovering on street corners and bus-stops,
raising and caring for our young,
	sponging down tarnished metal or kitchen china,
sweeping away the refuse and bile
of a million middle-class toilets.

Look how we reward these God-fearing subjects,
	these numberless multitudes, these massive minions.
Look at the resigned hopelessness of their eyes.
Che Guevera could never appreciate the power of the Papacy,
	the lure of redemption and an afterlife as pastoral
and perfect as a any nursery rhyme.
No matter, history makes no value judgments
	and power resides with those keen enough
to appreciate the vulnerability of the ignorant masses.
A city sleeps and dreams its reality.
Click the channel and there we are:
	laughing rosy-cheeked faces at Sunday picnics,
palm trees swaying in the summer sun,
fresh-cut lawns and manicured neighborhoods,
	patios with pools, porches with folding stools,
the smell of backyard barbecues,
an occasional car slowly whisking by...

Click the channel and there we are:
loud, grating car horns, police sirens,
screeching tires, burglar alarms, bolted doors

and slamming windows…
A sky so thick with smog the palm trees are hid
and the sun barely breaks above the horizon…

Years pass, a hundred, or forty or fifty. My years,
       the city half-imagined yet wholly real,
my years half-imagined yet wholly real.
A city dreams, the world turns in its continuum,
       the world and the city within the world,
the world and the words that echo light's language:
Visions of childhood, memories reclaimed
       in color and black-and-white.
The Hollywood skyline, the San Gabriel Mountains, the L.A. River,
working-class families, mothers, fathers, friendships, crazy uncles,
       movie palaces, movie stars, dive bars and beaches.
Memories reclaimed. A city captured in words. A world of words
captured in lamplight.

I look up at the lead-laced skies.
The shadow of 747 stretches across the arid landscape.

A taxicab idles and welcomes me home.

NOTES

The first epigraph by W. C. Williams is from the book *Paterson*, published by New Directions 1947.

The second epigraph by Lawrence Durrell is from the first book of the Alexandria Quartet, *Justine* published by E.P. Dutton 1957.

The Ithaca reference in the first section I feel is self-explanatory though a professor friend of mine suggested I would be better served in elucidating my intentions. The brown-stone habitat I reference is, of course, the time-honored establishment of Cornell University where the highly acclaimed novelist Vladimir Nabokov once conducted classes. The contrast of the mythical land of the same name in Homer's Odyssey, now turned gray and icy cold, while the sun-lit splendor of Los Angeles is meant to serve as a modern contrast to the Odyssey myth as viewed from my own myth-seeking eyes.

Why introduce Dante as an airplane passenger in the poem? I see this poem as both a Dantesque descent as well as a Homeresque odyssey. I thought it might be fun to inject some humor with *He reminds me how oppressive the heat can be when we make our descent./He seems to be an expert on that subject.* I'll leave it up to the reader to decide its relevancy or lack thereof.

"Vidal said to me…"of course, refers to Gore Vidal during a campaign gathering at his home in the Hollywood Hills. He was running for the California Senate seat against John Tunney. I was his investment advisor at Merrill Lynch. I was introduced to Kenneth Rexroth by my college mentor Ann Stanford at a faculty function in Northridge near the university campus.

Much of the facts highlighted in Part II can be verified from *Hollywood: The First 100 Years* by Bruce Torrance published by The Hollywood Chamber of Commerce 1983 and *Literary L.A.* by Lionel Rolfe published by Chronicle Books 1981.

Data contained in Part V can be verified by any of the Kevin Starr publications issued by Oxford University Press 1990.

Epigrapgh by Frank O'Hara in Part VIII is from *Lunch Poems* published by City Lights Books 1964.

Part XVI refers to the Watts Riots of August 1965.

The epigraph in Part XXII is from Homer's *Odyssey* translated by Richmond. Lattimore

Part XXVII, George Seferis, *A Poet's Journal: Days of 1945-1951* translated by Athan Anagnostopoulos.

The epigraph by Bukowski in Part XXXVII is from a Life Magazine interview 1989.

Part LI: "devil-may-care men who have taken to railroading out of sheer lust of adventure" from W. C. Williams' "To Elsie".

ACKNOWLEDGEMENTS

Grateful acknowledgement is made to the editors of the following periodicals, online journals and anthologies in which some of these poems first appeared : *Spectrum; Compass; Erotica Cafe; Visions & Voices; The Juice Bar; Edgar Allan Poet Journal; Men in the Company of Women: A Provocative Men's Anthology; Red Fez; The San Gabriel Valley Quarterly. Edgar Allan Poet Journal: Los Angeles Edition 2015.*

I wish to also acknowledged the following friends and mentors whose guidance and assistance with this effort proved invaluable and, without whose encouragement and support, this work could never have found its way to the printed page: Mace Morse, Apryl Skies, Carol Potter, Molly Bendall, Bart Edelman, Jim Daniels and especially B.H. Fairchild whose gifts as a poet and visionary continue to inspire and motivate my own humble literary pursuits.

ABOUT THE AUTHOR

J.R. PHILLIPS resides in Los Angeles, California. A graduate of California State University, Northridge where he studied writing under the guidance and encouragement of Shelley Memorial Prize winning poet, Ann Stanford. He received his MFA from the Los Angeles campus of Antioch University. He is the father of three children and makes his home in the San Fernando Valley.